Happiness Isn't Brain Surgery
100+ Practical Tools
To
Defeat Depression

By: Dr. Dawn-Elise "Doc" Snipes

Artwork and Cover Design by Mireia Carré Ferrer

Recovery & Resilience Publishing
1633 W. Main St. #902
Lebanon, TN 37087
RecoveryandResilience.org

First Printing: 2018

ISBN-13: 978-0-9862563-1-8

Ordering Information: Special discounts are available on quantity purchases by corporations, associations, educators, and others. For details, contact the publisher at the above listed address.

Contents

Introduction

According to the National Institute for Mental Health, 1 in 10 adults reports experiencing depression annually. If you are reading this, either you, or someone you know, is among that 10%. The goal of this book is to provide you practical, workable tools to help you manage your depression. It is my firm belief that each person's past has made you who you are. Even if you experienced tragedies or abuse, if you are alive, it has not broken you, it has shaped you. What you were equipped to deal with when you were 5 or even 15 is much different now that you are an adult. You have the power to choose. To choose to be happy. To choose to not believe the nasty, hateful things someone said about you. To choose to not let anger and resentment drain all of your energy. First, you need to understand what causes depression and the effects it is having on you.

Let's start with the causes. On a very basic level, depression is caused by an imbalance in your brain chemicals. However, if you have ever taken antidepressants, you probably know that just taking a pill won't fix it. While there are those of you who are born with chemical imbalances, most you develop them over time. Regardless of how the imbalance was created, depression creates a nasty, self-perpetuating cycle. Let's look at one example:

Sally is depressed. So depressed that she does not have the energy to get out of bed. She feels exhausted. The more she stays in bed, the more exhausted she feels. The more exhausted she feels, the less she cares about doing anything else---even those things she used to enjoy. After a time, she even starts feeling guilty because she just does not want to do anything with anybody.

In the above example, the more Sally slept, the more out of whack her circadian rhythms got. Additionally, the more she slept, the worse the quality of her sleep and her levels of cortisol, norepinephrine and serotonin (brain chemicals) started getting out of balance. The more tired she got (because she was not getting quality sleep) the less desire she had to do anything, which led to feelings of guilt and maybe shame on top of the depression. These feelings led to changes in her attitude and self-esteem which compounded her unhappiness and her chemical imbalances.

What things might you be doing that create a chemical imbalance? It is likely, if you are depressed, you are either emotionally or physically exhausted and/or are lacking the adequate building blocks to make the necessary "happy" chemicals. For those who are interested, we are mainly focusing on serotonin, norepinephrine and dopamine. Ultimately, the interventions are very similar. Emotionally, you need to do things to trigger the release of "happy" chemicals and limit the things that trigger your "stress/anger/fear" chemicals. Mentally, you can start changing the way you think about things and what you focus on, so you feel more empowered (less hopeless and helpless). Physically, you need to take care of yourself so your body can make the happy chemicals, rest so you have energy, and reduce any chronic pain that makes you irritable or disrupts your sleep or concentration. Socially, it is vital to have healthy, supportive friends you can count on. You are not meant to deal with life all by yourself. Spiritually, identify what is meaningful in your life, so you can live more in tune with your values (instead of doing what everyone else tells you to do.) Environmentally, well, your surroundings often represent how you feel on the inside. Additionally, sights and smells are some of our greatest memory triggers. Does your environment remind you of a happy time and happy places? Let's see what you can do to make it uncluttered, inviting and relaxing.

You must add in things that make you happy. What is 1 thing you can do right now to start feeling happy?

When you start freeing up energy in one area, it can be used in others. If you choose not to stuff your feelings and dwell on resentments, you will have more energy, and probably see improvements in your relationships which will have other positive effects.

Many years ago, Abraham Maslow theorized that you have a hierarchy of needs. Before you can focus on something at a higher level, you need to have the lower levels in check. The first, most basic level is that of biology. You need food, water, shelter and physical health. After all, a hungry, thirsty, homeless person who is in constant pain is not really going to have the energy or desire to enhance relationships or work on abstract things like self-esteem. Once you are physically stable and are getting your basic needs met, the second level is safety—physical and emotional. You need to be in an environment where you do not have to be on guard all the time—from physical or verbal/emotional attacks. That is easier said than done, because most people who are depressed find that their most vicious attacker is inside their own head. Yep. All of those tapes and negative comments that you replay in your head all the time make your own head a very unsafe place. The next level is love and belonging. Before you can really start forming and nurturing healthy relationships, you have to be okay with yourself, otherwise, you will probably just look for people to complete, validate or rescue you. This often starts with having a healthy attachment to a primary caregiver. If you didn't have that growing up, all is not lost, but you will have to learn how to love yourself unconditionally and trust yourself and (at least some) others. You will learn about attachment and relationships later. Working on self-esteem comes next. This is when you start really liking who you are---no strings attached.

All that being said, you have already probably tried a few things. Some have helped, and some have not. You are hoping to start feeling better...uhhh...now! This book is broken down into daily readings. Each reading is only a page, or three at the most, and provides you with a tidbit of information and activities to try. You do not have to do them in order. Think of it like a menu of activities. The goal of this series is not to replace therapy if it is needed, but to help you identify small changes can help you feel dramatically better. My suggestion is to start by reading all the way through the book once, stopping to do some of the exercises that seem more interesting or useful at that very moment. Then, go back and re-read the book taking it slowly. Each exercise and activity is intended to be implemented or tried over a week or so. If you are in counseling already, or start it while reading this book, these exercises can be processed with your therapist as well.

Helpful tip: Get a 3 ring binder and a set of dividers. Create the following sections: "Activities," "daily journal," "gratitude list," "self-esteem," and "tools." As you go through this book, you can keep your work organized. Activities are things you do that help you learn more about yourself. Your daily journal is something you will write in each day to help you see connections between things like your sleep, attitude, environment and mood. The gratitude list is just a list of things you add to each day to remind you that, despite hiccups, you do have things to be grateful for. Your self-esteem section will guide you through identifying what you like about yourself, what you want to improve upon and what things you are beating yourself up for that are really not that important to helping you have a rich and meaningful life. Finally, the tools section is for any activity that you do which provides you with a tool *that **you find** helpful*. There are a lot of activities (more than 100) in this book and you will not find all of them helpful. That is okay. Different people prefer different approaches. Your tools section will become your go-to section when you start feeling bad. Just like it is helpful to have a screwdriver handy when the handle on your kitchen drawer gets loose, these tools will be in your toolbox to help you fix your mood.

Assessment

What triggers or makes your depression worse? (Highlight all that apply)

Emotional Triggers: Guilt   Regret   Resentment   Anxiety   Anger   Jealousy   Stress

Mental Triggers: Pessimism   Taking too much responsibility   Overthinking   Being "foggy headed"

Physical Triggers: Poor Sleep   Pain   Sickness   Dehydration   Too much caffeine   Drug/Medication Use

Lack of exercise   Hormone changes   Getting physically worked up

Poor nutrition (Do any foods in particular help or hurt your mood?)

Social Triggers: Being around people who are…   Depressed   Critical   Happy

Getting into a disagreement with someone   Not getting approval from someone

Low Self-Esteem

Environmental: Being around unpleasant people   Clutter and disorganization   Noise

Not getting enough sunlight (seasonal affective disorder)

Pictures, smells and other reminders of things that make you feel sad or hopeless

When you are depressed, what helps you feel better, even if it only works for 10 or 15 minutes?

What are the reasons you want to start trying to work on your depression? That is, how will it improve your energy, productivity, health, relationships etc.

How can you address each of the depression triggers above? (You will add to this list, but start thinking about it now)

Emotional

Since you have gotten a book on depression, it is likely that you are more interested in at least starting by improving your mood. Getting adequate sleep, drinking enough water, eating a healthy(ish) diet and dealing with chronic pain are also all important to help you feel happier, but you will learn about those later. Emotional interventions address the emotions that keep you feeling depressed by helping you:

- Accept unpleasant emotions and improve the next moment.
- Prevent unnecessary unpleasantness.
- Add pleasant emotions to your day.

That being said, let's turn our attention to those feelings. All people have emotions. Feelings impact how you think and feel physically, and how you think and feel physically impact your feelings. The way you react to any event is dependent upon your personal reality and prior learning experiences. So, if you are in pain and didn't sleep well, your personal reality may be kinda grumpy which may cause you to think about and interpret things kind of negatively. For example, if I wake up after not sleeping well and my back hurts I can be kinda cranky, dread going to work and tend to focus on what is going wrong, instead of what is going right.

To complicate this, it is extremely rare to experience a simple, one dimensional emotion. Emotions are complex and composed of levels much like the earth. The crust, or most visible emotion, is often the emotion with which you are most comfortable. The underlying emotions represent emotions with which you are increasingly uncomfortable. For instance, you may be aggressive and lash out if you are afraid of letting people see that you might not be perfect or might need help. "I can do it. Just leave me alone!" Anger pushes people away but does nothing to resolve the underlying issue—you needed assistance and are afraid (for whatever reason) to ask for help. Once you have identified that the anger was just your way of trying to protect yourself, then the issues related to why you are afraid to show weakness can be dealt with. If you are angry and/or anxious for too long, you start to run out of gas and will start to feel depressed. You have not completely dealt with any situation until you have dealt with *all* of your feelings about it.

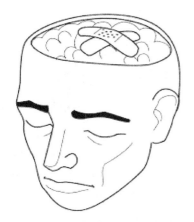

Let's start with stress. Stress is anything that requires energy---positive, negative, voluntary or involuntary---and you only have so much energy to go around. It is important to wisely choose how you spend your energy. Positive emotions (eu-stress) include feeling joy, elation, or confidence. Yes, even positive feelings require energy. Think about a really happy day in your life. You may have felt really awesome all day, but at the end, did you also feel a bit exhausted?

Unpleasant emotions (dis-stress) can be considered as all of the energy responsible for maintaining unhappiness. Distress not only includes depression, anxiety, anger and fear, but also the energy invested in constantly being afraid to feel those feelings, or keep them bottled up. You probably never really stopped to think about how much your moods affect your entire life: Mentally, socially, vocationally, spiritually and physically. When you are relaxed and "happy" you tend to require much less energy to get other things done. On the other hand, when you are unhappy, you may have trouble finding the energy to do simple things like getting dressed or even bathing. Note: Unpleasant emotions are there for a reason. They tell you there might be a threat or you might have lost something important or you might be unable to change something important. Embrace these emotions as a "smoke alarm" that is alerting you to the *potential* for a problem. Feeling them is natural and takes a bit of energy, but not a ton. What drains your energy is brooding, stewing and nurturing the negativity.

Emotional tools are those that are aimed at helping you identify your feelings, and feel them, while retaining the power to choose what, if anything, you are going to do with them.

Just because you feel a feeling does not mean you have to act on it.

Repeat that. What does that statement mean to you? How much more energy would you have if you chose your battles and chose to just let some things go?

All of your emotions are geared toward self-preservation. Pleasant emotions encourage you to do things again, while unpleasant emotions tell you there is a threat or concern.

Anger, resentment and fear are all protective feelings. They are designed to protect you from threats (real or perceived) to your emotional or physical wellbeing. When you are faced with a possible threat, your body activates the threat response system also known as Fight, Flee, Freeze of F***It. Fight= anger. Flee and Freeze= Fear. F*** It=Depression. When anger or fear is activated, your body starts dumping stress chemicals (adrenaline, cortisol, thyroxine). These chemicals increase your heart rate and respiration and start dumping energy into your bloodstream to give you the fuel to check if there is really a problem, and do what needs to be done.

Anger is a power play. It protects you and is designed to try and help you regain control of the situation by pushing people away like a bulldozer or helping you dominate the problem. Fear tells you to flee for your own safety. Freeze can sometimes be helpful if there is not an easy escape.

In theory, this is a great system, but there are a couple of problems. First, that energy has to come from somewhere. Your body diverts energy from cellular repair, digestion and your immune system in order to prepare you to fight or flee. In occasional instances, this is not a problem; however, when you are constantly angry or anxious, your body is constantly providing energy to fight or flee. This brings us to the second problem. Eventually, the fuel tank is empty. With no energy left, you start feeling "depressed." Usually this starts with fatigue, confusion, difficulty making decisions and sleep problems. "I sleep all the time, but I am exhausted" you say? Yes, you are, but like a soldier sleeping in a fox hole on the front lines, as long as your body perceives a threat, it will likely try and avoid a deep sleep so you can spring to action at any moment. Pain, lack of quality sleep, sickness and even your thoughts can make your body think it needs to keep the threat response system going.

In the big picture, if you are anxious or angry AND depressed, the depression may be a sign that you are out of gas. Your body is shutting you down for a while until it can restock, and it is saving energy for only the most extreme emergencies. This is the F***It response.

Most organisms (from rabbits to humans) will choose to flee instead of fight. It is the smarter evolutionary choice. When David faced Goliath, how likely was it (without divine intervention of course) that David would win in a fight with him? Unlikely. However, it was very likely that he would be able to successfully flee. Somewhere along the way, many humans started becoming control freaks, trying to control and fight things that are not controllable or winnable. It is vital to learn how to accept the things you cannot change and identify the things you can.

To do this, you need to get in touch with your feelings, thoughts and your ultimate goals. This will help you identify distress and choose thoughts and reactions that will move you toward your ultimate goals which will make you...guess what...happy! Feelings or emotions are natural events. Happiness, joy, excitement are all rewarding feelings. When something makes you feel good, you are likely to do it again. Depression can happen when you lose something important to you, or when you have been stressed or angry for too long and start feeling hopeless and helpless to change the situation.

Part of reducing the unpleasant feelings (which drain your energy and leave you feeling isolated, hopeless and helpless i.e. depressed), and increasing the positive ones is understanding what makes **you** feel each feeling.

Mindfulness

Mindfulness is the first step to becoming aware of how you feel, and what you want and need in any given moment (such as better sleep, something to eat or even a hug). It can also help you become more aware of your unhelpful thoughts and make choices that will help you move closer to your goals. Mindfulness can help you start to recognize your thoughts as just that...thoughts that can come and go, not reality. How often do you think about something you need to do, get up and walk into another room and forget what you had set out to do? Thoughts. I can have a thought about how awful something will be, but imagine it being a cloud in the sky that just floats on past, or I can imagine lassoing it and holding on for dear life. Which one takes more energy?

Activity: Turn off Autopilot

Daily Check-In: Keep a log twice a day of your feelings. Have everyone in your household to do this.

- Check-in with yourself each morning before work or school AND each evening before bed.
- Identify how you feel, why you feel that way (If there is actually a problem that is worth your energy, what you are going to do about it), and what else you need.

Date: _____

How I feel emotionally, mentally, physically, socially	Why I feel that way	Is this actually a problem worth my energy	What am I going to do about it	What else do I need physically, socially, environmentally?
Anxious Overwhelmed Tired Hungry Isolated	I have a project to get done and I don't want people to think I am a failure if I can't do it.	No. Failure is part of learning and success, and I will likely get it done without a problem	Focus on the things I have succeeded at. Try not to care about what other people think.	A good night's sleep, a good breakfast, a distraction free environment and a pep-talk

- You will NOT use the words fine (which is not a feeling anyway), happy, sad, mad, glad or afraid. Those are blah words that allow you to gloss over the intensity of the situation. Try words like content, elated, giddy, frustrated, enraged, overwhelmed... Search on the internet for "emotion faces," for posters with different feeling representations. If you are a visual person, it makes it easier to identify the feeling this way.

If you have children, post the emotion faces poster on the fridge. At breakfast, ask them how they feel and why. Help them find solutions if they are not feeling happy. Remember, we are not born with words to identify our feelings. The younger you can start kids learning this vocabulary, the better it is for them.

Activity: What Makes You Tick?

Feelings can be grouped into three broad categories: Anger, which includes rage, irritation, resentment, guilt (anger at yourself), and jealousy and envy (anger that someone else has something you want); Fear which includes anxiety, panic, worry and "stress;" and depression which occurs when you lose something precious to you in the form of grief, or depression which results when you have been angry or anxious for too long and are plumb out of gas, or if there is just no enjoyment in life. Start identifying how different things make you feel. Nothing is too small.

- Make a page for each of the following feeling groups:
  - Happy/Elated/Excited
  - Angry/Frustrated/Irritable/Resentful
  - Jealous/Envious
  - Sad/Depressed/Helpless/Hopeless/Grief stricken
  - Scared/Anxious
  - Guilty

- Set a timer for 10 minutes. Pick one of the emotion sheets and start writing different things that bring up that feeling in you. Repeat this until you have done all 6 feelings. (Hint: Save Happy for last so you end on a positive note!)

- Over the next week, each night, review your day and add to these sheets as needed. Maybe you were caught in traffic and felt irritated. Then you saw a bunny family and smiled.

- At the end of the week, review your sheets.

- How can you deal with things that trigger anger, frustration, jealousy, sadness, depression, fear, anxiety or guilt? Review your sheets and...
  - Cross off any that are not worth your energy (i.e. Getting all fired up at someone who cut you off in traffic. As my 3 year old pointed out...he can't hear you anyway.)
  - Identify any that you can avoid (i.e. Leave a little earlier or take a different route to avoid traffic jams)
  - For any that are left, identify something constructive you can do with that energy instead of nurturing the negativity.

- How can you make the things that trigger happiness and excitement a priority and do them more often?

*If you don't like making lists, you can make collages instead. Collages take more time, so give yourself an hour for each emotion and do one each day for a week. If you have kids, they can also do the collages.

You can also get a Jenga game and write the different feelings on the blocks. When your child pulls out a block, he or she reads the feeling written on the block and identifies something that makes him or her feel that way.

A third option, especially for younger children, is to play charades. Have the actor try to get his or her team to guess what emotion is being acted out. The game moderator may have to explain to the child what some emotions are by providing an example, like: "Hopeful... Remember what you felt like last year when you asked Santa for a bike?"

Feelings are your body's first response to tell you that you might need to do something. Unpleasant feelings are like a smoke alarm. Just because you feel afraid, doesn't mean the situation is actually threatening. First, identify your feeling; then thank your brain for alerting you, and decide if there actually is a threat.

Activity: Create a Rich and Meaningful Life

Before you move into exploring the functions of each emotion more in-depth, it is important to identify what is important to **_you_**. What people, things and experiences do you want in your life to make it happier?

For me: My family, my domestic animals, a comfortable house, a job I love that enables me to pay my bills and my health. If I have those five things I can be very content and happy. Now, if I happen to have a really nice house, a fancy car, fame, a million dollars and 500 amazing friends all the better, but I don't **need** those to be happy.

- If you woke up tomorrow and your depression were gone, what would it be like?

- What would be the same?

- What would be different?

- What are the 5 most important things/people to have in your life in order to be happy?

As you go through the rest of this book, you will regularly ask yourself, "Is this [thought, feeling, action, person] helping me get closer to or further away from the things that are truly important for me to have a rich and meaningful life. Consider this story...

An investor was at the pier of a small coastal village when a small boat with just one fisherman docked. Inside the small boat were several large yellowfin tuna. The investor complimented the fisherman on the quality of his fish and asked how long it took to catch them.

The fisherman replied, "only a little while. The investor then asked why didn't he stay out longer and catch more fish? The fisherman said he had enough to support his family's immediate needs.

The investor then asked, "but what do you do with the rest of your time?"

The fisherman said, "I sleep late, fish a little, play with my children, relax with my wife, stroll into the village each evening where I sip wine, and play guitar with my friends. I have a full and busy life."

The investor scoffed, "I am a Harvard MBA and could help you. You should spend more time fishing and with the proceeds, buy a bigger boat. With the proceeds from the bigger boat, you could buy several boats, eventually you would have a fleet of fishing boats. Instead of selling your catch to a middleman you would sell directly to the processor, eventually opening your own cannery. You would control the product, processing, and distribution. You would need to leave this small coastal fishing village and move to the City, then LA and eventually New York City, where you will run your expanding enterprise."

The fisherman asked, "How long will this all take?"

The investor replied, "15 – 20 years."

"What then?" Asked the Mexican.

The investor laughed and said, "That's the best part. When the time is right you would announce an IPO and sell your company stock to the public and become very rich, you would make millions!"

"Okay, once I make millions – then what?"

The investor said, "Then you would retire. Move to a small coastal fishing village where you would sleep late, fish a little, play with your kids, relax with your wife, stroll to the village in the evenings where you could sip wine and play your guitar with your friends."

After reading that story, what adjustments might you make to your goals and the way you spend your energy?

Yesterday is history. Tomorrow is a mystery. Today is a gift, that is why we call it the present. - Alice Morse Earle.

The Function of Emotions: Protection

Now you will start learning about how each emotion is designed to protect you, and ways to address them in order to conserve energy and feel less hopeless and depressed.

Remember anger is the "fight" part of fight or flee. You feel angry when you feel threatened for some reason and you are trying to protect yourself. Fear, worry and anxiety are the flee part of fight or flee. The things that make you angry or scared usually fall into one or more of 4 categories: Rejection/Isolation, Failure, Loss of control/The unknown, Death/Loss.

- Example: You start dating someone and you are spending a lot of time together. Now, when you are apart, or when he does not call when he says he will, you feel anxious.

- Analysis: You may be fearing rejection (I thought he liked me. I wonder if I am not good enough?), failure (All my friends have great boyfriends and I cannot keep a guy interested), the unknown (I wonder if he is thinking about me or has moved on to someone else), loss of control (I cannot stand not knowing what is going on) and isolation (I haven't felt this way in a long time. If he leaves, I might be alone forever).

Reducing the amount of time you feel threatened will help you increase calming chemicals like serotonin and GABA, which will reduce your stress hormone, cortisol, helping you get better rest and feel more energized which will all help to relieve your depression.

Throughout the rest of the book you will be asked to identify what threats your unpleasant emotions are related to, consider whether that threat could keep you from achieving a rich and meaningful life as you defined it, and decide what the best use of your energy is so you can feel empowered instead of helpless and spend your energy on those things that are actually meaningful to you.

Anger & Anxiety

Anger and anxiety are the feelings you experience when faced with a threat.

Activity : Goals of Anger and Anxiety

Write down the last 3 times you got angry or scared.

- What was being threatened (self-esteem, your person, your reputation, your efficiency, something or someone you love, your finances...)

- Who or what (including your Higher Power if you have one) were you angry at or afraid of?

- What was the goal of your reaction in each situation? That is, in what ways did you want to make something happen or push someone away so he, she or it couldn't hurt you anymore?

- How do anger and anxiety impact your mood? Does it make your depression worse or better?

- Review your sheet and decide whether those things are worth your time, energy and happiness. If not, make a decision to learn how to accept the feeling and let it go. (It is possible. It just takes practice.). Try saying to yourself "I am feeling really angry/anxious right now, but staying upset isn't going to change anything. To improve the next moment I can _____"

Activity: Understanding Threats (What triggers your anxiety or depression)

Threat of Rejection and/or Isolation

- People are wired to be part of a group, not hermits on a desert island. It is natural to crave connection and have the desire to be loved. Some people like more connection than others, but it is likely that you want some. You also need to be accepted by yourself. When you reject yourself you are essentially living with a bully 24 hours a day.

- What types of situations involving rejection or isolation make you feel anxious, fearful or angry? (This can be anything from someone giving you a dirty look, to a neighbor or co-worker that doesn't seem to care for you much, to a break up or loss of a relationship, to not getting a job you apply for and everything in between)

- Why do you fear rejection or isolation in this situation from this person?

- What is the evidence for and against this fear?

- Is it realistic to expect to be accepted by everyone all the time? (Hint, the answer is no!)

- If this person doesn't like you, or this relationship ends, what are the likely consequences?

- Who in your life accepts me?

- In what ways do you love and accept yourself?

- In what ways do you reject yourself, and how can I address that?

- How else can you deal with this fear? (Think about what has worked in the past for you, or what seems to work for someone else.)

- How would addressing your fear of rejection reduce your depression?

- How would addressing your fear of rejection impact your relationships, your energy, your ability to concentrate and get things done?

Threat of Failure

Success = power and a sense of usefulness. In our society many people are judged based on what they can do...what they succeed at.

- How do you feel about failure? Does it mean you are weak or incompetent or is it an opportunity to learn and grow?

- What types of situations involving failure make you feel anxious, fearful or angry? (This can include a relationship failing, not getting a job you applied for, failing at something you try to do, etc. You will notice that things that trigger fears of failure and fears of rejection often overlap.)

- Why do you fear this? That is, what does this failure mean about you, and what are the actual consequences?

- What is the evidence for and against these fears?

- Is it realistic to expect to be succeed at everything all the time? (Hint, the answer is no!)

- In what ways can failure be a learning experience?

- Who do you love and respect that has failed at something?

- What do you want a child to understand about failure?

- How else can you deal with this fear? (Think about what has worked in the past for you, or what seems to work for someone else.)

- How would addressing your fear of failure reduce your depression?

- How would addressing your fear of failure impact your relationships, your energy, your ability to concentrate and get things done?

Threat of Loss of Control/The Unknown

- Some people are more control freaks than others, but when you feel out of control your brain will activate the "threat response system." Loss of control includes not being able to control what someone else does, says or thinks about you; not being able to control situation like a job interview; getting lost; dealing with a chronic illness or even waiting for test results.

- If you would call yourself a control freak, what are you afraid will happen if you are not in control? How likely is it that the worst case scenario will happen

- What types of situations involving unknown and loss of control make you feel anxious, fearful or angry? (These can include driving in an unfamiliar place, flying, rain on a day you were supposed to go hiking, waiting on test results, not being able to reach someone by phone, asking someone out etc...)

- Why do you fear this?

- What is the evidence for and against this fear?

- Is it realistic to expect to be able to know and control everything all the time? (Hint, the answer is no!)

- When in the past have you been in situations that you did not have control, or did not know exactly what to expect and everything turned out okay?

- When facing a situation in which you do not have total control, how can you deal with it? (For example, at a job interview or on a blind date)

- What things do you have control over in most all situations? (Hint: Your reaction, your safety, your behavior)

- By accepting responsibility for only what you can control, how can that help you feel less hopeless and hopeless? How will this reduce your depression?

- How else can you deal with this fear? (Think about what has worked in the past for you, or what seems to work for someone else.)

Threat of Death or Loss

- The grief process includes denial, anger, bargaining, depression and acceptance. It is natural to get angry then depressed when you lose something or someone important to you.

- You can lose things, lose people, lose hope, lose dreams, lose control and lose self-esteem

- What types of situations involving death and loss make you feel anxious, fearful or angry? (Fear of dying, fear of losing a significant relationship, loss of self esteem, loss of hopes and dreams, loss of dignity (embarrassment), etc.)

- Why do you fear this?

- What is the evidence for and against this fear?

- Is it realistic to expect to never experience losses? (No!)

- While it is painful to experience a loss, how can you deal with it? (Hint: Accept that better things await, remember the good things about the person or thing, learn from the experience, etc.)

- How would addressing your issues surrounding death and loss reduce your depression?

- How would addressing your issues surrounding death and loss impact your relationships, energy, and ability to concentrate and get things done?

Putting It Together

- For the next week, when you start feeling an unpleasant emotion identify which threats are triggering fear for you and why. (Remember the threats are Rejection and Isolation; Loss of Control and the Unknown; Failure; Death and Loss)

- Once you have identified all of your fears and self-statements related to the situation (as in the example), go back and identify which ones are just blown out of proportion or not based in any fact. Cross those off. Finally, for any that are left, identify how you can deal with those fears.

- At the end of the week, review all your entries. There should be at least one entry each day. Are there any themes? Do you have particular fears, like fear of rejection, that seem to happen a lot? What do you need to do to address that?

- What can you do to start feeling good about yourself regardless of other people's opinions, confident in yourself even if you are not in control all the time and proud of yourself, even when you fail at something?

Resentment

Resentment is a form of anger, but instead of aggressively pushing people away it creates a barrier so nobody can get close. For example, I resent when people try to manipulate me. Unfortunately, that causes me to pay more attention to, or be more suspicious of, people's motives, creating that barrier. Resentment can cause you to feel helpless, hopeless, less grateful for what you have and depressed.

Activity: The Impact of Resentment

- Go back to that list you made of things you resent.

- How does resentment impact your relationships, your sense of peace, hope and faith in the world?

- What benefit are you getting from holding on to resentment?

- How can you forgive or accept the situation so you are not continuing to waste your energy?

One way to start dealing with resentments right now is to make them *specific to that person, situation, place and time*, learn how to prevent them when possible and decide how to deal with them. Instead of saying "I resent that people never consider my feelings," saying "I resent that John didn't consider my feelings last Thursday when he cancelled our plans at the last minute."

In the example above, I recognize that the people in my past who have manipulated me did not have my best interest at heart. I continued to hope I was wrong and do things that I didn't really want to do. That caused me to feel angry all the time, lose some self respect (temporarily) and negatively impacted every other area of my life. By making my resentment <u>specific</u> to those particular people or situations, it helped me not be as guarded with everyone. I accept that, while most people are good, there are people out there who will get upset when they cannot manipulate me, but I am okay with that. Holding on to resentment toward people in my past harms nobody but me. They certainly aren't thinking twice about it. It is important to learn from my mistakes and move on. Anger shortens my lifespan. They are not worth losing another second.

Guilt: Anger at Yourself and Energy Tied Up in the Past

Guilt is anger at yourself, and comes from an Old English word that means "delinquency." Today Merriam-Webster's Collegiate Dictionary defines it as "feelings of culpability, especially for imagined offenses or from a sense of inadequacy; self-reproach." It's a revealing definition — nowhere does it say that guilt is related to things you _actually_ did wrong.

Sometimes you should feel guilty (if you've done something morally wrong, committed a crime, or intentionally hurt someone). But if you're like most of us, you walk around feeling guilty because of all the "shoulds" that come into your life that are imposed by other people. Pay attention for a week to how many times you tell yourself you "should" do something and then do it, but resent it, or don't do it and feel guilty about it. That's not only bad for your mental and physical health, but completely unfair to you. Constantly feeling guilty is exhausting and contributes to a sense of hopelessness, helplessness and depression.

What can guilt do to you?

- Make you become over responsible, striving to make life 'right'. You may overwork, give too much of yourself, or be willing to do anything in an attempt to make everyone happy.

- Make you over-conscientious. You may constantly worry about how every action you take may have a negative consequence on others.

- Immobilize you. You can become so overwhelmed by the fear of doing, acting, saying, or being 'wrong' that you are paralysed from doing anything.

- Interfere in your decision making. It may become so important to always be 'right' in your decisions that you are unable to make a decision because you are afraid it might be wrong.

- Codependency. You begin supporting or enabling another person's poor choices by doing things for them that they can do for themselves or covering up for their mistakes and protecting them from natural consequences.

- Cause you to be unable to feel the full array of emotions and feelings available to you. Guilt can make you unable to enjoy the positive things in life, because you are always focused on the negative.

- Mislead or misdirect you. Many unhelpful thoughts lead to guilt (taking things too personally, thinking in all or none terms or ignoring other people's part in the situation). Be objective when you are experiencing guilt so that your decisions are based on sound, logical thinking.

- The benefit....Guilt can be a motivator for change. Guilt and the discomfort it brings can indicate a need for change and a encourage you to do something differently (for the better),

Activity: Guilt Pack

Review the list of things you feel guilty for.

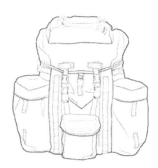

- Get a bunch of stones or bricks. Have count how many guilts are on your list and add that many weights to your pack. (This is great to do with kids too.)

- Put on the backpack and carry it around while you do housework or yard work.

- Think about how much guilt weighs you down and zapps your energy. How much harder is it to just get up off the sofa carrying all that weight?

- Next, identify which guilts you can either forgive, fix or let go and how (You will learn strategies next). You can take those weights out of their pack.

Activity: Fix It and Forget It.

Correct any mistakes you can. If it is something you should feel guilty about, you need to figure out how to deal with it. Many times, the things we feel guilty about are relatively easy to make right such as doing something to make amends like saying "I'm sorry." Continually beating yourself up only hurts you and does nothing to fix the situation. If you threw a ball through someone's window, feeling guilty about it wouldn't fix the window or repair the relationship with the person whose window you broke. Instead, repair the window and apologize.

Whenever you feel guilty, ask yourself, "How can I repair the window?"

Activity: Right and Wrong.

Just because you have a feeling of guilt doesn't always mean that what you did was wrong. For instance, if you're feeling guilty because you decided it was more important to relax with a book than to have coffee with your always-in-a-crisis friend, that means you're learning to set limits and take time for yourself. In cases like this, you are hearing those "should tapes" in your head that are critical and demanding. Ask yourself if what you did was the best choice in that situation to make sure you were using your energy to move toward those people and things that are truly important in your life. If so, then you probably made the right choice. What is right and wrong is rarely simple.

Activity: Get A Second Opinion.

If you are not sure whether what you did was right or wrong, talk to a relative or friend about your guilt. Often your own memories are not the most accurate; your feelings of guilt may be coming from something that really didn't happen the way you remember it, or you are not considering all the factors. For example, my son's dog, Kenny was left out in the fenced yard that was about 800 ft. from the road. He jumped the fence and ran an out into traffic after a cyclist and got killed. For the longest time I focused on the fact that Kenny was left unattended and felt terrible guilt. In retrospect, the yard was fenced and waaaayyyyy off the road. He had never jumped the fence before, and the woman who hit him was speeding excessively on a residential road. Do I still feel a little guilty sometimes, yes, but I also recognize that there were a lot of other factors and feeling guilty won't bring Kenny back.

Activity: Start A Guilt Journal.

Every time you feel guilty about something, write it down in your journal. Write the time, the day, what you feel guilty about. Go back and reread this journal every couple of weeks to find the trends in your guilt. This will provide clues to the sources of your guilt that will enable you to better deal with its underlying roots.

Activity: No Guilt Allowed.

Set a no-guilt-allowed rule whenever you go on vacation or do something just for yourself. Often you may not experience vacations, breaks, and other relaxing activities as stress-relieving because you feel guilty that you are not doing more productive things. Tell yourself that you are taking a break and doing it for a reason (improved health, decreased stress, recharge so you can be more productive etc.), so there is no reason to feel guilty. As soon as you hear yourself say, "I should be…" remind yourself why you are _choosing not to_ do that. For more on this topic, google Stephen Covey's 7th habit: Sharpen the saw. You are much less effective if you are run-down.

Activity: Bill of Rights.

You may have grown up in a home in which boundaries, especially emotional ones, were not respected. You learned that if someone is sad, you need to be sad too, and you may even need to fix it. Emotional boundaries allow you to separate your emotions (and responsibility for them) from someone else's. It's like an imaginary line or force field that separates you and others. Healthy boundaries prevent you from inappropriately giving advice, blaming or accepting blame. _They allow you to protect yourself from feeling guilty for someone else's unpleasant feelings or problems, or taking others' comments personally._ Healthy emotional boundaries require a clear awareness of your feelings and thoughts.

If you feel anxious that someone will be mad or think less of you or feel guilty (angry with yourself) for setting boundaries, remember, your relationships suffer when you're unhappy. This anxiety or guilt probably stems from being taught as a child that it is not safe or acceptable to set boundaries and that you should always put other's needs and wants first. It will take your family and friends a bit of time to get used to your new assertiveness, but once you get practice setting boundaries, you will feel empowered and less anxious and resentful. That will ultimately improve your relationships and your happiness.

Currently, you may not know what your rights are. For example, you have a right to privacy, to say "no," to be addressed with courtesy and respect, to change your mind or cancel commitments, to ask for help, to be left alone, and to turn off your phone and electronic devices after work hours.

Creating a personal bill of rights will help you remember what you have the right to and what your boundaries are.

- Think about all of the things you feel guilty doing or not doing. These often represent places where your boundaries are weak. Make a chart with your guilts on the left and your rights on the, well, right. This will become your personal bill of rights.

- Think about all the situations where these rights apply. Write how you feel and how you currently handle them. How often do you say "yes" when you'd like to say "no?"

- Write want you want to happen.

Guilt	Bill of Rights
Sleeping in on Saturday	I work hard all week and there is plenty of food for the kids to make their own breakfast. I have the right to sleep in.
Going to the gym when my in-box is full	I have the right to take care of myself. (My in-box is always full, and I will be more effective if I clear my head).
Not answering the phone.	I have the right to choose with whom and when I share my energy.

Guilt takes a toll on self esteem and can leave you feeling unlovable---which is depressing. When you feel less guilty, you will have more energy for fun, feel lovable and less depressed. Boundaries mean setting limits on what other people expect of you and ensuring you get your own needs met without feeling guilty.

Jealousy

Jealousy and envy are anger at someone else or your higher power for something you do not have. In the short term, these feelings can motivate you to do something to get what you want, like go back to school so you can get a higher paying job, or try out for American Idol so you can be the next famous singer. Like anger though, these feelings are not helpful if you just nurture them, by doing things like watching Lifestyles of the Rich and Famous and just being unhappy that it isn't you.

Activity: Jealousy/Envy

- Who or what are you jealous of?
- Can you have a rich and meaningful life without this thing?
- What do you currently have that makes your life rich and meaningful?
- Is it something you can possibly have? (If not, then being jealous is just going to suck your energy dry).
- What would you need to do to get it?
- Is it worth the energy it would take to get it?

Grief

Grief is a label you assign to all of the emotions associated with dealing with a loss. Grief indicates you lost something important to you.

The grief process actually occurs in phases. First you deny that it happened and may try to convince yourself it is a bad dream. Then you may get angry that it is happening. After this you may try to figure out ways to get it back. When you finally realize that you cannot get it back, you may enter a phase of feeling helpless and hopeless (depressed). Different people go through these phases at different rates and often go through each phase more than once. You may have difficulty resolving grief because you get stuck in the anger or depression phase.

Once you get past denial, you have to face some very scary realities which may make you feel angry. Anger either dominates the problem or pushes it away. It may protect you against the six basic fears: fear of failure, fear of rejection, fear of loss of self-control/respect, fear of isolation, fear of death, fear of the unknown. It protects you emotionally, physically and socially by keeping you from feeling afraid. It gets you out of threatening situations (ideally), and it alienates you from other people who could cause you to experience fear or harm.

Many people fail to identify the threats (Yes, those again!) underlying the anger in the grief process. Without coming to terms with these threats, it is much harder to "resolve" the loss. Once you have identified the source of the threats or danger caused by the loss, then you can choose the best way to deal with it. It is important to remember that death is not the only loss to be grieved.

The final stage in the grief process is acceptance. Learning to live with the loss. Think of it as the end of a season of your favorite show, or a chapter in a book. That storyline has ended.

Activity: Losses

The following are different types of things that can be grieved. In what ways have you experienced losses in each area?

- Hope
- Faith in yourself, others or the world.
- Dreams
- Friends/People/Pets
- Self-Esteem
- Sense of safety
- Money/Things

Activity : Grief and Acceptance

Go over your list of losses and start working on dealing with them by identifying:

- Why it was important to you.

- What threats (rejection, failure, the unknown, loss of control) it triggers for you.

- What you have control over now.

- How it changed you.

- How the loss made you stronger?

- What good memories do you have of it that you can hold on to?

Emotion Management

Now that you have an idea about what types of things make you feel unhappy, it is important to understand the impact of those emotions on you and identify tools to manage them.

Activity: What is that Smell

As an adult, you may not need to do this, but if you have children or adolescents in your house, this activity really drives home the point.

- Get a bag of something really stinky (a baby diaper or dog poop is great)

- Put it in the living room and label it "Anger and Negativity"

- As your family comes in see how they react. (They will probably be looking around to try to find it and get rid of it, or figure out who to blame it on.)

- Then pick it up and try to get close to someone with it. (They will probably move or lean away).

Then process the following with them...

Think of unpleasant feelings like dog poop. If you let poop sit in the living room, eventually the smell will permeate the whole house. Likewise, you wouldn't bag it up and carry it around with you all day. No. Not only is that unpleasant, but it would repel other people. When you smell the poop, you know you need to get up and see if the dog actually crapped on the floor, or if he just farted. If he crapped on the floor, then you need to do something to address it.

Unpleasant feelings are the same way. When you feel them it's merely a signal to get up and check out the situation to see if there is a problem. If there is, do something about it so it doesn't permeate your whole life. You wouldn't bag poop up and carry it around with you all day...

- Why then do you carry negative feelings around with you?

- How do negative feelings affect your entire day?

- Your relationships?

- What could you do instead?

Activity: Ride the Wave.

Feelings are there to tell you to pay attention. Nothing more. Nothing less. Feelings are NOT facts.   I had a snake in my house the other day. My initial feeling was one of anxiety. My brain was telling me it *might* be a dangerous situation. I stopped and took a breath and realized that it was a harmless garter snake. I was afraid for a moment, but then realized there was no factual basis to it. Most feelings occur and crest within about 5 to 10 minutes. They only continue if you decide to give them power by dwelling on them or nurturing them.

Find a video of waves (surfing videos are good). Wind blowing over the water gets it all stirred up creating a wave. More wind provides more power and creates a bigger wave.

- What is your wind? That is, what fuels your emotional wave?
- When there isn't enough wind to sustain it, the wave dissipates. What do you do to maintain or reduce your emotional wave?

One thing you can do when you feel a feeling, but do not want to get stuck in it is ride the wave. This means, identify what you are upset about, accept your reaction (It is what it is), check it out to make sure there is no immediate threat (there usually isn't), and then do something else. This gives you time to let the adrenaline drain off so you can think more logically about the situation instead of nurturing the unpleasantness and being blinded by adrenaline.

Make a list of:

- 10 things you can do to distract yourself when you are fearful/anxious/worried
- 10 strategies to help when you are angry or resentful
- 10 things to do when you are feeling depressed.

Keep this list with you to refer to when you are feeling upset. Remember that too much fear, anger and resentment often cause (or at least worsen) depression.

Activity: Commitment.

Part of dealing with depression is recognizing that, while some things in your life may suck at the moment, there are still other things that help to make it rich and meaningful. Those are the things you are committed to using your energy on. Listen to the song from The Sound of Music, "Raindrops on Roses." In it, Julie Andrews is singing about simple things (which we often overlook) that can help you feel happier. Even if you do not have a lot of negativity in your life, if you do not have things that make you happy you will feel depressed. Try to make your own version of the song. Example:

Bright sunlit mornings, and cool breezes blowing

Seeing my house clean, or going out mowing

Amazon packages left at the door

Life on the farm who could want any more….

When the dogs bark, when the phone rings when I'm feeling sad,

I simply remember my favorite things, and then I don't feel so bad.

Activity: Make Lemonade.

We all have different things we enjoy as well as dislike. Part of being happy is not only doing things that make you happy, but also minimizing those things that don't. Realistically, there are some things you do not like that you will still have to do (like laundry), but you can try to make those things more tolerable. When things are less unpleasant, they take less energy. This leaves more energy for positive things.

There are a few strategies that can help you make unpleasant tasks tolerable.

- The easiest is to pair them with something you like. I hate folding clothes, but with two kids it is an inevitability. So, when it is time to fold laundry, I put on some of my favorite music (loudly) and rock out. When it is time to do socks, we set out 4 laundry baskets and try to throw the paired socks into the correct basket.

- When I was working on my dissertation, there were parts that I hated. My committee chair suggested "Do 15." I was to work on it for 15 minutes each day. If, at the end of 15 minutes, I still could not get my head in the game, I could go do something else. Most of the time, I found that getting started was the worst part. I have since used this for housecleaning, exercising and getting clinical notes done.

- The third option is to give yourself a reward after you do whatever it is. For example, after you finish paying bills, do something enjoyable—watch a movie, play with the dog, eat that last piece of chocolate cake. The key to rewards is to make sure they are rewarding to you, and to get them right after the task. For most of us, saying, "If I do _____ all week then I can _____" is a great thought, but the reward is too distant, and we don't make it until Friday.

Make a list of things you have to do, but do not like, and use at least one of the options above to make each activity more pleasant. (Bills, folding or ironing laundry, dishes, exercising, Christmas shopping, yardwork, driving to the office…)

Serenity

In the addiction recovery field we have something called the serenity prayer. It says---

Grant me the serenity to accept the things I cannot change

The courage to change the things I can, and

The wisdom to know the difference.

Too often the people I work with exhaust a ton of energy trying to change things they have no power to change. This ends up leading to all kinds of unpleasant emotions. Consider the following example: If I were to tell you that, if you go outside and do 1000 pushups it would stop raining. If you want the rain to stop, you might go out and do it. (Stay with me here.) After about 10 minutes of doing pushups, how do you feel? Exhausted? Irritated at me for wasting your energy? Hopeless, because this was supposed to fix the problem and it is still raining?

You have the knowledge and the power to identify those things that you can change. Choose to save your energy for those things instead of wasting it trying to control something that you have no ability to control.

Before even trying, you knew you couldn't control the weather. Don't use all your energy and get exhausted fighting a losing battle. If something causes you distress, then figure out what you can change. For example, my house faces east/west, so I have sun and heat pouring into the house all day. I would love to pivot the house 45 degrees to make it more energy efficient, but that isn't possible. What I can do to make the house more energy efficient is get tinted windows and plant fast growing trees outside.

When something is bothering you the first step is to figure out what the problem is and what solution you would like. (I wanted lower electric bills). The next step is to identify which parts of the situation you can influence to achieve your goal. (I couldn't move the house, but I could take other steps).

Oh, and why are you irritated at me? You are the one who chose to go out and do pushups, knowing good and well it wouldn't stop the rain. As you become more self-aware, you may find that you get angry at other people for how *you* feel and what *you* do. Most of the time people can't *make* you do or feel anything. It is your choice. For example, I could get irritated at the people who built my house for not facing it in the most energy efficient direction, but...what good would that do? I knew what direction the house faced when I bought it. Being irritable would just drain my energy and impair my relationships.

Hopelessness often goes hand in hand with powerlessness. Nobody likes feeling powerless, but when you continuously try to change and control those things that you cannot change, you are setting yourself up for failure, powerlessness and depression. I would bet you would be surprised at how often you try to control the weather.

Activity: Serenity

In this exercise you will:

- Review the list of your current stressors and irritants

- Identify which ones of those you have the power to change, and what you can do to change them.

- For those you do not have the power to change, how can you change the way you feel about them? Let it go? Look at the bright side? View it as a learning experience? Remove yourself or that stressor from your life?

- The final step is to do it, which takes courage. What are you afraid of? What is holding you back from changing those things you can? Make a plan to deal with at least one thing on your list each day. (Keep this list going forever. It will help you be mindful of your feelings.)

Hints:

- You cannot change other people, only the way you react to them and whether or not they are a presence in your life.

- Likewise, you will always occasionally have unpleasant feelings. Remember that is your mind's way of protecting you. You do have a choice about what you do with those feelings (carry them around with you like smelly dog poop, or do something to improve the next moment).

- Finally, there are somethings that cannot be changed. It is important to figure out how to have a rich and meaningful life despite that fact.

Find Your Inner Child (AKA Take Off the Fun Filter)

I am not sure who keeps telling everyone that once you grow up you must be serious and stodgy, but it cannot be further from the truth. When I was working in a residential facility, this became abundantly clear one day when a patient came up to me and said, "Everyone here looks so stressed and miserable, if that is what recovery is about, I am not sure I want it." That comment has stuck with me for 20 years. It was true. My staff was overworked, underpaid and burned out. I set about trying to figure out how to fix it, right then and there. Don't get me wrong, there is a time and a place to be a grown up, but how devastating is it to always be so serious? Learn how to find your inner child.

Activity: How to Be a Kid

 Start by making a list of things you liked to do as a kid. If your childhood was less than enjoyable, what did other kids do, or what would you have liked to do? Fly kites? Play in the mud? Play in the sprinklers or on a slip-and-slide? Build forts? Color? Try to work these into your life at least 3 times a week. Yes. I am almost 50 years old and I still love to watch cartoons, swing on the swingset and play on a slip and slide.   After my son was born, I would regularly be walking (half skipping) through the halls at work humming "Goober Peas" or "Honker Ducky Dinger Jamboree." Try putting a basketball hoop on the back of your office door. One of my employees got clown shoes, a clown wig and a lab coat. When he sensed that things were getting too tense, and people were taking things too seriously, he would don his costume and come strutting out of his office. It was his way of just saying "chill out people."   Just like kids have to behave all day at school, you may have to adult when you are at work. After work though, what would a 10 year old you want to do?

Activity: Play Date

Set aside a day just to be a kid, and not feel guilty about it. If you have kids or someone willing to play with you, that will make this much more fun. Sleep in. Don't make your bed. Watch cartoons all day. Make a blanket fort in the living room. Eat cereal for every meal. Go to the beach and build sand castles or look for shells. Go to Wal-Mart and play Marco-Polo in the aisles. Hula Hoop. Go to the roller skating rink. Get a book of knock-knock jokes and don't be afraid to laugh at them. Whatever it is that helps you get in touch with that inner 10 year old—DO IT!

- What was your favorite show/cartoon?
- What was your favorite food?
- What was one of your favorite songs?
- What was different when you were little that you miss now?

The **next** day, write a journal entry about the effect being a kid for a day had on you. Did it help you unblock your creativity? Did it give you a new perspective on something? Do you just feel more relaxed? Is it something you will start doing monthly?

Part of being a kid is to be silly and not caring what other people think. Visit a park sometime. The little kids are not thinking---"What will people think if I…" They are just having fun. They have not yet developed their fun filter. My daughter walked up to me the other day and proudly announced "Listen Mommy, I can burp like a trucker!" Sure enough, she could. Is that ladylike…errr…no. Did it make her laugh? Yes. Laughter releases endorphins. Laughter at yourself not only releases endorphins, but prevents some of those negative, critical thoughts and accompanying stress chemicals.

Belly Laugh

If you cannot laugh at yourself, then you probably think you need to be perfect. Nobody is perfect, so you are setting yourself up for a sense of hopelessness (depression) and failure. (Trying to be perfect is like trying to change the weather).

Laughter is one of the easiest ways to release natural happy chemicals. You read earlier about laughing at yourself, but that is not usually a truly heart-felt belly laugh.

- Laughter relaxes the whole body. A good, hearty laugh relieves physical tension and stress, leaving your muscles relaxed for up to 45 minutes after.

- Laughter boosts the immune system. Laughter decreases stress hormones and increases immune cells and infection-fighting antibodies, thus improving your resistance to disease.

- Laughter triggers the release of endorphins, the body's natural feel-good chemicals. Endorphins promote an overall sense of well-being and can even temporarily relieve pain.

- Laughter protects the heart. Laughter improves the function of blood vessels and increases blood flow, which protects you against a heart attack and other cardiovascular problems.

Activity: Daily Laughter.

Set aside time to laugh every day for a week. It does not have to be long, maybe 15 minutes a day, or on your ride to and from work (if you are listening to a comedian).

Find a comic book, cartoon or other material that makes you laugh. Try the Far Side, Calvin and Hobbes, Garfield---but remember, a chuckle is good, but we are aiming for a belly laugh—if it makes tears come to your eyes, then all the better. I love Grumpy Cat and Snark E-Cards.

Explore different comedians. Jeanne Robertson, Bill Engvall, Jeff Foxworthy, Robin Williams, George Lopez, Dennis Miller or Jeff Dunham to name a few... I am sure you can find one or two that strike your fancy. Make a playlist of your songs for your mobile device. Happiness at your fingertips.

Download joke apps on your phone. I usually aim for the knock-knock jokes, because they are appropriate for all audiences, but use your discretion.

The Art of Distraction

Sometimes life just sucks, and there is nothing you can do about it. You have every right to feel your feelings. Grief is one of those feelings that many people get stuck in. When you lose something or someone, likely there is nothing you can do about it. You feel depressed, like someone kicked you in the gut. There is no way to put a happy spin on it. It just is. What is more annoying is that people keep saying it will get easier with time, but you are suffocating NOW!

Distraction is anything you do to temporarily take your attention off a strong emotion, because sometimes, focusing on a strong emotion can make it feel even stronger and more out of control. (Like watching the doctor give you a shot.) By temporarily distracting yourself, you may give the emotion some time to decrease in intensity, making it easier to manage. When you are grieving or feeling any of the unpleasant emotions, sometimes you need a break just so you can breathe. It does not mean you are not devastated anymore, it just means you are giving yourself permission to regroup—like your own personal half time. Distraction is not about trying to escape or avoid a feeling forever, it is a tool to help you reduce the intensity of the feeling so it is easier to see options for how to deal with the situation.

Activity: Distraction Inventory.

Make a list of 15 things you can do to distract yourself. Examples: Read a book, go on a walk, call a friend, organize your closet, play with the dog, change locations, exercise. In extreme cases, you might even hold ice cubes. I can pretty much guarantee if you hold ice cubes in your hands until they melt, you will not be thinking about much else. Keep this list in your wallet or on your mobile device so it is with you when you need it.

Activity: Your Happy Place.

When you start getting upset, make a conscious effort to go to your imaginary happy place. Take 20 minutes and imagine the most relaxing, amazing place. Describe it. What are 5 things you see? How big are they? What color? What type? What else do you notice about them? What are 4 things you hear? How loud is it? Is it high or low pitched? What is making the sound? What are 3 things you smell? What do those smells remind you of? What does it feel like (hot, cold, breezy etc...). You get the idea. Really try to mentally transport yourself there. Your happy place is somewhere you can go when you need to escape. It can be helpful to narrate this and record it, so when you are feeling stressed, you can put on your headphones and be transported to your happy place. (Windows has built-in sound recorder, as do most mobile devices.) You can also look for videos online of nature sounds like rain, babbling brooks or ocean waves that can serve as background noise during your mental vacation.

Activity: Start a project.

When I need a distraction I start designing something for my garden, or envisioning some type of home improvement project. This takes 100% of my focus, so whatever it is that is bothering me tends to fade to the background. Make a list of 2 or 3 projects you want to do, so when you get upset, you have something on which to focus. Include mindless projects like cleaning out the upstairs closet or rearranging the garage too. Some days you may not feel like taking on something complex.

Okay, a brief recap...

You are keeping a daily log of your feelings to learn more about what makes you tick, developing strategies to choose how to use your energy, surrounding yourself with more things that make you happy (pictures, music, pets, smells etc.), scheduling in time to be a kid at least 3 times a week, and, on your way to and from work or while you are doing house chores, you are listening to something that makes you laugh. Got all that? Good!

Cognitive

Cognitive interventions help you address the way you think and can change how you:

- Perceive situations—Do you look at the positive or negative? How do your past experiences impact how you react to or interpret situations?

- Receive information. Are you a detail person? Do you remember things better if you read them or hear them?

- Encode and retrieve information. Your brain is like a great big filing cabinet. How do you store memories? Sometimes, like files, your memories can get stored in ways that are too general. Instead of looking at the particular person or situation, you may simply start sticking most everything into the "You Suck" or the "This is Dangerous and Scary" file.

- Solve problems. Sometimes you need to get out of the box. If everyone around you is negative, depressed or unmotivated, it may seem like a leap to say—"Hey, let's try this…" Sometimes that is just what is needed to get the momentum started in a positive direction.

By making small changes in the way information is interpreted and remembered, it is often possible to change the way you feel about situations. As your good feelings increase, the effects on the whole system are mind-boggling. You can concentrate better, make better decisions and problem-solve more effectively. You'll have increased immunity, better quality sleep, fewer physical complaints, and, above all, more available energy. You may also tend to be more positive and notice more of the good things.

Let's start at the beginning. As you go through life, every interaction is experienced, interpreted and filed for later reference. These files are called schemas. These schemas help you know how to react based upon past experiences. The first time you saw a traffic light, you developed a schema about it. You learned that after it is yellow, it will turn red. Now when you see a traffic light that is yellow, you call on that schema and know what to expect. Unfortunately, you do not automatically update like your computer when things change. The way you interpreted an experience when you were 10 will likely impact how you react to a similar experience when you are 30, unless you consciously update that schema with the facts that you are older, more independent and have new skills and tools that you did not have back then. For example, when you were a kid, strangers were probably scary, as was staying home at all night by yourself. As you got older if you learned that strangers weren't that scary and staying at home alone could be pretty fun. You updated your schema. If you didn't update your schema, you would still be afraid of those things.

As you get new information, your brain has to do something with it. Jean Piaget called these activities assimilation and accommodation. Assimilation is using an existing schema to deal with a new object or situation. Accommodation happens when the existing schema (knowledge) does not work, and needs to be changed to deal with a new object or situation. The following activities will help you start helping you understand assimilation and accommodation to make your thoughts work for (instead of against) you.

Perceptions: "Life is 10% reality and 90% what you make of it."

No two people are exactly alike. For that reason, no two people perceive the same situation exactly the same way. From birth, you take in information and fit it into schemas (expectations of the way the world is). You form schemas about, and assign meaning to, people, places and events based on these past experiences. Schemas shape your reaction to and interpretation of the world, because they act as filters through which information is processed. When information is new or unexpected, you have to either: 1) Do some creative remembering to make the event fit into what you expect (assimilation), or 2) your expectations (schema) have to change to fit the new information (accommodation).

Everything You Know

Schemas allow you to predict what will happen next. Remember that schema about stop lights? From past experiences you learned that after a stop light turns yellow, it turns red. If there was a glitch in the system and the light went from yellow to green, that would be unexpected.   You would have to either assimilate that occurrence into your current schema--"I must have daydreamed through the red-cycle" or accommodate your schema to fit the situation--"Sometimes yellow lights will turn green." In general, if your schemas (expectations) are negative, that is, if you see the world as a generally hostile and dangerous place, you will likely always interpret things with a negative twist. When I ask is the glass half full or half empty, which do you choose? When I say is it partly cloudy or partly sunny, what do you say?

Perceptions are exactly what they sound like, how you perceive the world based on your schema. This is why two different people can perceive the same exact situation in very different ways…Some are afraid of snakes, dogs, flying, or someone making large hand gestures, while other people may have a positive reaction to those things.

There are three dimensions on which we base our perceptions: Internal/external, global/specific, stable/changeable.

Let's start with Internal vs. External. This is where you perceive that life is controlled from. That is, do you believe that you control your own destiny (internal) or that you have no control over your life and everything just happens to you (external). When something happens to you or someone else, do you believe that it is because of something you or they did, or was it just destiny?

Activity: Internal or External

Read the following statements. Place a 1 next to every statement with which you agree and a 0 next to every statement with which you disagree.

_____ I believe that I control my own destiny

_____ I believe that much of what happens to me is beyond my control

_____ When I make a mistake, I look at what I could have done differently

_____ I blame other people for making me unhappy.

_____ When I see someone fall, I assume they are clumsy

_____ When a friend is late, I assume he or she got delayed

_____ Generally, our environment determines who we are and what we do

_____ The environment has an impact, but I can choose how to think and behave

_____ Most criminals are good people who are products of bad environments

_____ Most criminals are evil and have no regard for anyone else except themselves

_____ I believe in a predetermined fate or destiny

_____ There are consequences to every action which constantly change my destiny

Results: This was a brief survey designed to evaluate how much you believe you have control over your thoughts, feelings and behaviors. More statements in the "Internal" category means that you believe you have control over what happens to you. A high number of "External" statements mean you have a somewhat helpless sense, and you attribute the cause of most things to environmental causes beyond your control.   Ideally, you will have marked some statements in each category.

"You have brains in your head and feet in your shoes, you can steer yourself in any direction you choose!"
--Dr. Seuss

Internal: 1, 3, 5, 8, 10, 12   External: 2, 4, 6, 7, 9, 11

In reality, you want a balance. Too internal and you are going to try to control things that are uncontrollable. Too external and you may fail to take action to change the things you can.

- Review each statement above. Think about how interpreting each statement in an extreme manner has the ability to increase or decrease stress and identify the middle ground.

Example Statement: I believe that I control my own destiny

- Increases stress by placing a lot of responsibility on you for making the right choices and can unnecessarily burden you when factors beyond your control do affect your life.

- Decreases stress by empowering you to take control and not feel like you are at the whim of an unseen force.

- Middle Ground: Not everything is within my control, but I do have the ability to shape my life by acting on those things that I can change.

How can you improve your perceptions to improve your health and happiness? For example, do you take too much responsibility for things that you only have partial control over? Do you not take enough initiative to change things you could?

Global or specific is the next dimension. If you often overgeneralize, then you probably have more global perceptions. For example, if you make a mistake at something and call yourself stupid, that is a very global statement. A more specific statement would be, "I made a stupid error on that report." Another example is "I have no sense of direction. I cannot find my way out of a paper bag." A more specific statement would be. "I have difficulty finding places in big cities." See the difference?

- Pay attention over the next week at how often you use global statements like "I am…" "You are…" "That always…" and change them to more specific using words like in this situation, sometimes, often, and some things.

Stable or changeable is the third and final dimension. Some things, like the color of your eyes are stable. Other things, like how you choose to interact with other people are changeable. Albert Ellis says that there are only two things that you cannot not do and that is to be born and to die. You have a choice about everything else. He recommends that his patients replace the word "can't" with the word "won't" or "choose not to" as those words are much more accurate. He also advocates for removing words like "should've", "should" and "ought" and replace them with more active words like: "choose not to" and "will." By changing the way you speak, you are reminding yourself what things you have the power to change.

- To summarize, over the next week, when you feel unhappy, identify the cause of the situation. Make problems specific. Finally, identify the things you can and cannot control.

ABCs

The ABCs have been used for many years as a method of anger management. The goal of this method is to help you identify your automatic (and often unhelpful) thoughts and ways of reacting to situations. Once they are identified, they can be better dealt with. It is possible to apply this coping method to just about any feeling or reaction.

The basic structure is as follows: Fill in "A" activating event and "C" consequence first.

- A= Activating event or the stimulus (What happened?)
- B= Your automatic (and often unrealized unhelpful Beliefs)
- C= The consequence of those beliefs (What was your reaction?)
- D= Determine if your beliefs and your consequences are rational/constructive.
- E= Evaluate whether the situation is worth the energy of continuing the reaction

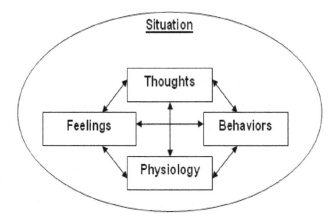

Example: Sally is upset because she got a bad grade on a math test.

- The Activating event, A, is that she failed her test.
- The Belief, B, is that she must have good grades or she is worthless. Getting bad grades is the worst thing ever.
- The Consequence, C, is that Sally feels depressed.
- When Sally moves on to D=Disputing she will (hopefully) realize that there is no evidence that she must have good grades to be worthwhile, or that getting bad grades is awful. She wants good grades, and it would be good to have them, but it hardly makes her worthless.
- This leaves her with E= Evaluating whether the situation is worthy of continued energy. She cannot change that grade, but she can improve for the next test. Getting bad grades is disappointing, and it means she may be currently bad at math or at studying, but not as a person. She may feel disappointed, but this momentary disappointment can be a healthy

motivator. Instead of beating herself up over a grade she cannot change, she can use that energy to address her study habits or get a tutor.

Activity: ABC Worksheet

I feel _____about (state the event) _____

- Why do I feel this way? (State the first belief) I am having the thought that...
- Is this accurate, based in facts and helpful? Yes/No   Why?
- Why else do I feel this way? (State the next belief) I am also having the thought that...
- Is this accurate, based in facts and helpful? Yes/No   Why?

Repeat the above statements until all the reasons you feel how you feel are stated and defended. Then evaluate the reaction.

- Is getting upset about this situation the best use of my energy? Yes/No.
- If not, how could I use my energy to change the situation or improve the next moment?

Complete this worksheet at least once a day for a month to become more mindful of your automatic thoughts and reactions and start learning to choose how to use your energy.

Cognitive Distortions

Albert Ellis said that when you evaluate the "beliefs" in the ABCs (see the previous activity) you will often find that they represent unhelpful (irrational), automatic thoughts. Unhelpful thoughts can be identified because they often contain the words: should, should have, must, cannot, or indicate that an event would be completely unbearable, or the worst thing in the world. These types of statements often spawn unnecessary worry or guilt and prevent you from recognizing your own ability to make choices.

The following is a list of some of the most common irrational thoughts:

1. I must have love, approval and affection from everyone almost all the time

2. In order to be worthwhile, I can't make mistakes

3. People who make me feel bad are mean and should be punished

4. If I do not get my own way, awful things will happen.

5. Unbearable misery comes from all of the demands other people make on me.

6. If something is dangerous or scary, I can't help but to dwell on it.

7. It is easier to avoid than face life's difficulties.

8. My past must continue to determine my feelings and actions today.

9. It is awful if I do not find quick solutions.

Activity: Unhelpful Thoughts.

Write a sentence or two disputing each of the common unhelpful thoughts above.

- Example: I must have love, approval and affection from everyone almost all the time
- Reality: I cannot please everyone all the time, nor can I please anyone all the time. Expecting to do so puts me in a position to feel powerless and hopeless. I can love myself all the time, even if I don't always like my choices or behaviors.

Activity: Thinking Errors

Write down 3 examples of how you have made yourself miserable with each of the following thinking errors.

Arbitrary inference: Making assumptions without all the facts

- **Example:** You assume that because your roommate didn't come home last night that she must be dead in a ditch somewhere.
  - ◦ **Solution**: Ask yourself---Do I have all the necessary facts? Are there other possible explanations?

Selective abstraction: Only seeing what you want (or do not want) to see

- **Example:** You think your best friend is the greatest when, in reality, she breaks promises, lies and uses you.
  - ◦ **Solution:** Try to force yourself to look at the positives and negatives to keep a balanced perspective. Get other people's input.

Over generalization: Generalizing things about one situation to all similar situations

- **Example:** The head cheerleader is not nice, so all cheerleaders are mean.
  - ◦ **Solution:** Look for exceptions. Find cheerleaders who are nice.

Magnification and exaggeration: Blowing something out of proportion when it really wasn't that big of a deal.

- **Example:** You have a really bad headache and assume it must be an aneurism and you are going to die. Or, you were having company over for dinner and burned the entrée.
  - ◦ **Solution:** Ask yourself how likely it is that the worst thing is going to happen, or that this event will destroy life as you know it.

Personalization: Feeling like everything is either your fault or a personal attack.

- **Example**: My boss gave me a dirty look, so I must have done something wrong.
  - ◦ **Solution**: Look for 3 alternate explanations. (Maybe he is having a bad day or spilled a drink.)

Polarized thinking: All-or-nothing.

- **Example:** She always throws me under the bus. He never cleans off the bathroom sink.
    - ○ **Solutions:** Look for exceptions to this statement.

Pay attention to these defeating thought patterns and eliminate them from your life! When you get upset, always remember to check for these unhelpful thinking patterns.

Create an emergency card with the following questions:

- Do I have all the facts?
- Am I basing my reaction on feelings or facts?
- Am I seeing the whole situation?
- Am I using moderate words like sometimes, occasionally or often?
- Am I making sure not to devote too much attention and energy to something that really won't matter in a few days or weeks?
- Have I considered possible explanations besides it being all about me?

Shoulds: Who Said?

Many people are absolutely miserable because they are doing, feeling and thinking the way they think they "should." It is a travesty that we do not do more to encourage children to be inquisitive. When kids are about 2, they go through the "Why?" phase. Unfortunately, most of the time what they hear is "...because I said so!" or "That's just the way it is." This teaches them to not think, just to be passive receptacles of information.

As you grew up, you may have failed to question everything (or anything) you had learned while growing up. Why is the sky blue? Why do dogs bark instead of meow? Why do we need to be the best, the brightest, the richest or the strongest? Why am I expected to be okay with this?

Activity: Should List.

Make a list of the things you were taught when you were growing up. Identify who said that and then whether you believe it is still true. Use the format below.

Example:

- Should: I should keep a clean house at all times, so people do not look down on me.
- Who Said: My mother
- Alternate belief (if any)? A clean house is not the ultimate priority, and needs to be balanced with other life demands.

- Should: I should just say "Yes ma'am" even when my boss is lying and knowingly manipulating me.
- Who Said: My old boss
- Alternate belief (if any)? It is important to pick your battles, but I do not have to tolerate being lied to and intentionally manipulated.

- Should: I made a commitment, so I have to see it through 100% of the time
- Who Said: My parents, my friends (who in reality do not fulfill their commitments 100% of the time either)
- Alternate belief (if any)? Things change and sometimes commitments must be given up. It is not right to hold myself to a higher standard than I hold everyone else.

Optimism and Cognitive Restructuring

Some people believe that optimism is an inborn personality characteristic while others believe it is a learned behavior. Regardless of your viewpoint, optimism is a behavior that can be learned. By viewing the glass as half-full instead of half-empty you can save yourself a lot of needless worry. Optimism is way of changing the perception of a situation.

Worry and regret are two by-products of pessimism that drain your energy, make you feel hopeless and helpless and serve no functional purpose. Worry is energy tied up in the future, and regret/ guilt is energy tied up in the past. Nobody can predict the future with any accuracy, nor can they change the past, so why let your thoughts dwell there? Just choosing to take a more optimistic view is sometimes sufficient. Other times, it also requires a behavior change. For instance, maybe you are concerned about getting cancer or AIDS. If you spend all your time worried about getting sick, you will drain yourself of energy and decrease your natural immunity, increasing the chances of getting sick. You will enjoy life a lot more if you look at situations optimistically: 1) Right now you are healthy, 2) the cures for these diseases may not be that far away, and 3) if you take reasonable precautions, you will lessen your chances of getting sick.

Now, if you had an oozing lesion on your back for three months, the worry is well founded, but still will serve no functional purpose. That energy must be used instead to make an appointment and get to the doctor. Most of the time when you procrastinate, it is because you are putting off something you either do not like or something that frightens you. This is where optimism comes in. If you look at a visit to the doctor and see it as ominous, then you are going to have a hard time motivating yourself to go. If, on the other hand, you see the doctor's visit as a means of getting early intervention for something that is entirely treatable, then it becomes a more "do-able" task.

Likewise, regrets are in the past and there is nothing (yet) you can do to change the past. Therefore, you must view it as a learning experience and move on. Moving on can mean anything from simply not dwelling on something that cannot be changed, to actually doing something constructive in the present to alleviate that regret and/or make amends.

Activity: Optimism

Write down several (10) situations about which you have worry or regret (or review the list you already made), then write an optimistic restatement.

Example:

- Worry: I am worried that my children are going to grow up with a lack of self-discipline and work ethic.
    - ○ **Restatement:** Right now they are testing my boundaries and being kids. They have good role models and need a little bit of freedom to find their own rhythm.
- Regret: I regret that I did not study harder in my college calculus and chemistry classes.
    - ○ **Restatement:** I was taking those classes premed and I would not have been happy as a medical doctor. I love what I do and make a difference in my own way.

Activity: Flip a Coin

Another way of changing your perceptions is to change your attitude. Have a positive, attitude of gratitude. With practice, you can train yourself to start seeing more of the positive in life which can help alleviate depression.

- Each morning for the next week, when you get up, flip a coin.
- If it lands on heads, you must spend the entire day seeing the positive or optimistic side of things (fart rainbows). If it lands on tails, behave just as you would normally.
- At the end of the day, write a journal entry or spend 15 minutes thinking about how your day went.
- At the end of the week, evaluate to see whether having a more positive attitude freed up some energy and made things go more smoothly.

Activity: Journaling or Drawing

At the beginning and end of each day spend 5-10 minutes thinking about, writing about or drawing a picture of all of the good things that will happen or did happen that day, and things that made you smile. Include the obvious things like...

- Morning: I woke up on time. I feel energetic. It is a beautiful morning. Everyone is healthy. I'm looking forward to my morning coffee. I have a lot to do at work, so the day should go fast.

Today is leg day at the gym (Yes, that is a good thing!). I woke up to a really interesting show about animals. Today is an opportunity to make it the best day yet.

- Evening: I got to work safely. Lunch was really delicious and I enjoyed visiting with Sam. The day really did go by quickly. I had a good workout. My family is safe and content. I got paid. I saw a mama deer and twin fawns. I love the smell of the new fabric softener on my sheets...

You get the point. After a week, look back over your notes. Identify things you could add to make your days even better. For example, I will get some black oil sunflower seeds and put them in my bird feeder so the birds come more often. I will also splurge and get the really good coffee at the store. ☺

The research shows that after 30 days, most people experience improvements in their mood that last all day.

Self Esteem

Self-esteem is simply the way you feel about yourself. It is the product of your evaluation of your real-self compared with your ideal-self. Everyone has an ideal-self. This is who you believe you should be. (Remember, "shoulds" almost always add unnecessary stress). You formed this schema of the ideal-self at an early age based upon what people said you "should" be. That is, as a child, praise was given not for who you were, but what you were able to do or how you were able to act. As a result, you formed schemas or ideas about what a "good girl" or "good boy" should be.

Due to children's immature reasoning, many things are overgeneralized and made into global, stable and internal attributions. They start to think… "I have to be [this way] all the time or I am a bad person." This tends to create an unrealistic ideal-self. For instance, many girls grow up with media influences that show women who do it all, and they are told (directly or indirectly) that to be good enough, they need to be attractive and successful partners, mothers and business-women. This is called the superwoman stereotype. The same types of influences make little boys believe they must always be strong, successful, good partners and primary providers. In reality, it is nearly impossible for either gender to do all of those things all the time. Your real-self is who you are with all of your inherent imperfections. Your self esteem is how you feel about yourself when you compare the "Me I should be" with the "Me I am." You may see that you have room for improvement. That is actually a good thing. You can always improve. When you look at your real-self the "Me I am," how do you feel about that person?

To improve self-esteem, you must look at all of the things on your "Me I should be" list. Identify which ones are really important to help you have a rich and meaningful life. Then comes the hard part. For the things you decide are less important, cross them off and change the way you feel about them (that is, realize that it is not important to you to be good at everything and you are loveable without that characteristic). For example, I may never be able to run a 24 minute 5k again or be as thin as I was in college, but neither one of those things is critical to helping me have the life I want right now.

If it is something important then you need to make a plan to change yourself. For example, being a loving and available parent for my kids is central in my vision of a rich and meaningful life. Because of some health issues, working out like I used to could kill me. So, I will stop trying to push my limits at the gym so I can be there for my kids.

Activity: Self Esteem Activity

- Describe your ideal self.

- Review it and cross out any characteristics that are not really that important to you. Example: I would like to be in the top 2% of women in terms of my physical fitness, but just because I am not doesn't make me less lovable.

- List all of the personal attributes you have of which you are proud.

- List all of the good/nice things you have done for other people in the past month

- What is your biggest fault?

    ◦ Why is this a fault?
    ◦ In what ways does this keep you from being who you want to be?
    ◦ What can you do to correct this problem
    ◦ When considering your faults, ask yourself whether it is really a fault or just something someone may have said to you that stuck (i.e. you're fat, you can't do math. . . .).

Activity: Add in the Good

Here are some good qualities which you might consider trying to add. Focus on adding only one every week or so, because it is not easy to do them right. See which ones help you feel happier and less stressed.

- Highly efficient perception of reality based in fact and the ability to take multiple perspectives and be objective.

- Acceptance of strengths and weaknesses in self and others

- Naturalness and spontaneity: flexible and comfortable with yourself

- Commitment and dedication. Say what you mean and mean what you say.

- Appreciation for the present moment: random acts of kindness, "stop and smell the roses"

- Creativity

- Brotherly love which is the genuine desire to help the human race.

- Democratic character.

- Integrity, a strong sense of personal ethics.

- Sense of humor.

- A sense of being at peace with oneself and one with the world.

Activity: Affirmations

Make a list of positive affirmations and add one new one each day. You can also do this as a family activity by making an affirmation jar or notebook for each person. Everyone in the family writes an affirmation to everyone else each day.

Examples

I am smart. I am loyal. I am funny. I am a good person. I am loving. I am creative. I am in good physical shape. I am kind to animals. I am enthusiastic. I am determined. I am a hard worker. Nobody can make me feel inferior. I inspire others. I am brave. When I fail, I will fail forward. I am lovable just as I am.

Activity: Fault Balancing

This week, whenever you find a fault in yourself, remind yourself of three positive qualities. Pay attention to your self talk.

Activity: Give Me Credit

Do not minimize your positive actions or accomplishments. This week, take credit where credit is due. When you do something nice or extraordinary, take credit for it. Don't minimize by saying "It was no big deal." "Anyone would have done it."

Activity: Positive People

Surround yourself with people who are positive and encouraging. My best friend in college was a ball of enthusiasm and positivity. Nothing was every just "okay." It was always "fabulous," "splendid" or "amazing." Just being around her made me feel good. Positivity and love are contagious. Who in your life is positive? Who brings out the best in you? Spend more time with them (even if it is just talking on the phone or on social media).

Activity: Self-Improvement

Instead of complaining about faults, take positive action. Identify the top 3 things about yourself that you want to be different. Pick one. Make a plan to change it. For example, I am not as patient as I would like to be. That is something I can actively work on. As you start making positive changes you will feel more empowered (less helpless) which will help lift your depression.

Activity: Change What You Can

If there is something you feel "bad" about that is impossible to change, then add a new, positive quality. Think about the cliché of the person who makes up for a lack of physical attractiveness by having a good personality. Maybe you have a chronic illness that keeps you from being able to do all of the things you want. Since you cannot get rid of the illness, what positive quality can you add?

Activity: Good Deeds

Do a good deed every day. It will help you feel happier and bring happiness to others.

Activity: Have Patience

Changes do not happen overnight. When you start wanting to be the ultimate you, remember that all good things take practice. Focus on how far you have come already. Review your daily check-ins to see your progress. Are you more often feeling happy, focused, motivated, rested, healthy and loved?

Activity: Double Standard

Evaluate whether you hold yourself to a higher standard than you hold everyone else. Do you think you are that much better than everyone else, or do you just need a reason to beat yourself up? Be reasonable with yourself. When you start being self critical, ask yourself if you would criticize your friend or your child for this.

Activity: Get over yourself

Although not mentioned in the thinking errors, you may make yourself miserable because of something called the availability heuristic. That is, when you do something, it is very present in *your* mind, and you can be reminded of it regularly. However, other people who watched you do that, have probably long forgotten, or they were too consumed with their own stuff to even notice. Of course, there are a few that are really funny, but that is when laughing at yourself becomes so important. Shame, embarrassment and guilt may all be present here. For example, there was one time I accidently tucked the back of my dress into my stockings and walked down the hall at work with everyone being able to see my hiney. I was mortified. While it felt like **everybody** saw and would remember **forever**, only a few people actually did see, and they forgot about it in a few days.

Activity: Dealing with Embarrassment

- What things have you done in the past that you are still embarrassed about today? To identify some of these things, try completing the following sentences (If you cannot, then great...no shame there, but if you can, it may be impacting your self esteem, relationships and mood.)

  - You must think I am such an idiot because...
  - I cannot believe that I...
  - You must think I am the worst person in the world because...
  - I can't face you after I...

- Why are you embarrassed or ashamed about these things? What do they say about you?

- If your best friend did the same thing, would you still be holding it against her/him?

- Do you believe that you are what you do? That is, do you believe that if you do bad things then you are bad, or do you believe that you just messed up?

- If you are embarrassed or ashamed about what you did for a reason (maybe making a scene in a restaurant), then learn from it. Write down how can you handle it better the next time? Otherwise, cross it off the list. Nobody (but you) cares.

- If you want to test this theory, ask people if they remember one of the incidents. Do not provide a ton of details. Most of us can remember stuff if we are prompted enough. Say something like "Jan, do you remember that time I freaked out at that party?" If it takes her a few minutes to remember, then. Voila, you have your answer. If you would not have brought it up, she probably would have never remembered it at all.

Sometimes embarrassment can keep us from forming healthy friendships. Since healthy relationships are all but essential for stress management, then without them you can feel isolated, overburdened, helpless, hopeless and ...depressed.

Time Management

 Time management seems to be one of the most elusive and devastating of all the coping skills. When you don't manage your time well, it can lead to poor evaluations at work, friends getting mad at you or failing to take care of something important. All of these things can lead to you feeling bad about yourself, guilty and depressed.

Activity: Time Management

- How does poor time management affect your life? Your relationships?
- When you are distressed because you have too many things to do and not enough time, how does it affect you? Do you feel exhausted? Overwhelmed? Powerless?

The amount of time spent and the amount of energy expended are not the same thing. You probably spend a lot of time doing things you enjoy, but, because you enjoy them, the tasks do not use much energy. Unfortunately, if you are spending a lot of time doing things you enjoy when there are other things pressing, you are going to have to double or triple your energy output to accomplish the less desirable tasks.

- Identify a personal example of when you have spent a lot of time, but not a lot of energy on something.
- Example: I can spend a lot of time reading the news in the morning which means I have to work faster to get ready for work and the gym.

The following is a list of several of the most common time-management styles. You may be a combination of styles. Figure out which one or ones you fit into and ways to address the problems.

Activity: Type A

If you are Type A, you are plagued by a sense of time-urgency, hostility and often misdirected anger, poor organizational skills and a tendency to take on multiple tasks simultaneously. You often strive for perfection in everything, which often leads to doing many things poorly instead of doing a few things perfectly. When things do not go as planned or are imperfect, Type As tend to take it personally which contributes to feelings of helplessness and hopelessness. The other result is that you become a person who, although you accomplish all of your goals, and complete them with high quality, neglect the other areas of your life. This can lead to feeling unfulfilled, lonely and depressed.

1. You hate the idea of wasting time so you do things the moment they come to mind. You always have too much to do and not enough time to do it. To address this, ask yourself...

- What MUST be done?
- What would actually happen if some of the things on your list didn't get done?

2. You have trouble understanding the stupidity of others. You don't believe yourself to necessarily be exceptionally gifted but believe that "If you want it done right, you need to do it yourself." Instead, think about...

- What things can you delegate?
- What is the worst thing that will happen if it doesn't get done the way you want it done?

3. You often become passionate about things they do. All of the things you do. This is why you often start getting irritable. Everything is important, and it is impossible to get everything done.

- Make a list of the important things in your life and prioritize them so you can have laser focus on one or two of your passions.

For example, I am passionate about animal rescue, gardening, working out, being a mother and teaching. I cannot possibly do all of those things whole heartedly at the same time. I have to prioritize. I do more animal rescue in the spring during kitten and puppy season because my garden needs less attention. I do more teaching and writing over the winter when I do not want to be outside in the garden. I focus on my gardening from June to September.

4. Because you are so passionate, and because true success takes patience, any sort of early failure easily discourages you.

- How can you pace yourself, so you don't run out of gas half way into the project?
- How can you deal with failure in a way that helps you grow and be even more successful at the task?

5. You're prone to stressing and being irritable. You do your best to see into the future and can't shake the fact that things can always go wrong. Since you are passionate about what you do, this make you dread that ever possible and looming, crappy outcome.

- When you start worrying about the future, identify what you are worried about, the facts for and against that belief and whether that outcome is likely and probable or a one in a million chance. (Is it worth getting worried about a one in a million chance?)
- What things can you do to make sure that you have done everything you can to ensure the success of the task? (Once you have done that, there is nothing more you can do.)

6. Although you know you should take more time to relax, you don't find it appealing – plus, you simply can't find the time. You feel most at home working and doing your thing. It's difficult for you to understand that getting away and slowing down is in your (and everyone else's) best interest.

- Try an experiment. For one month, pick a day each week to relax and unwind. Try to do a whole day, but if you just can't manage it, do 8 hours. Plan on doing something fun with friends, or just vegging out with a good book. Write in your journal how you felt at the end of that day. Also write in your journal how you feel the next day. (I usually feel more energized and excited to go to work if I took a day off). Many times, relaxation helps you recharge, unblock your creativity and remember all of the other things that are important in your life.

7. You love sleeping, since being passionate about a bunch of things all the time is exhausting, but you have trouble stopping your thoughts from racing.

- Review the section on sleep and start developing a sleep routine.
- Incorporate 30 minutes or an hour of non-work, non-task related activity that can help you get out of the traffic of your mind. (I play scrabble/words with friends or watch television and crochet)
- When you notice your mind start to race, write what you are thinking about on a notepad, so you can tend to it the next day.
- Avoid naps. They will disrupt your circadian rhythms.

8. For Type A's, things always need to be done. You are able to focus intently and block out the rest of reality. You may call it getting into your "zone." Unfortunately, when someone dares interrupt the zone, they are usually in for a tongue lashing. This can cause problems in interpersonal relationships.

- How can you let people know you are in your zone and not to be disturbed?
- How can you schedule your "in the zone" times to mesh with the schedules of other people in the household? For example, my "in the zone" time is from about 6am-1pm. I try to avoid appointments during this time. I spend time with my family after 2pm. Likewise, when I am

working out, I am in my little zone. I have my headphones on and my family knows that I shouldn't be disturbed unless it is an emergency.

9. Doing things efficiently is your first priority—spending as little time getting as much quality work done as humanly possible.

- Efficiency is great, but you miss a lot of things. What would happen if you took a more relaxed pace. I am the queen of multitasking, but that also means I often miss out on subtle issues and appreciating the moment.

10. You are a perfectionist. It's not that you are trying to be perfect, but blemishes, mistakes and inconsistencies frustrate you. They find them ugly and appalling.

- There is a point of diminishing returns. Somethings you want to be completely perfect, but for most things, nothing would change if they were slightly imperfect. You only have so much time. Is it worth all the time for re-proof a report multiple times to make sure there is not a comma out of place?
- The person who graduates medical school with a C average is still called doctor.

11. You make plans, lots of plans. Unfortunately, making plans isn't always efficient, because they take a lot of time to create and often need to be adjusted (or scrapped). Since Type As like plans and structure, when things don't go as planned it greatly increases your stress.

- Before doing something, think about what you want the end goal to be and then get started.
- If things go wonky, be willing to drop back and punt. Getting upset will only drain precious energy.

12. You have a tendency to cut others off in conversation -- not to be rude, but to be right. What's the point of letting them yammer on with some nonsense when you can just tell them the way it really is, and then you can both move on with your lives, right?

- Practice active listening.
- Try to think about how they could also be right.
- Remember that assertive communication means recognizing that everyone's thoughts and feelings can be valid.

13. You believe that always having a plan for the worst-case scenario is a necessity. What's the worst possible thing that you can possibly imagine happening to you? Losing your job? Your dog getting run over by a car? Cancer? Armageddon? Yup, you already have a plan for that.

- Practice mindfulness. Focus on what you have in the present, not all the things that could go wrong.
- Identify which parts you have control over.
- Use your energy purposefully to protect and care for what is most important to you. Once you have done your part, it is up to the powers that be.

14. You walk fast and with a purpose, doing all you can to avoid lines of any sort. To you, walking is getting from point A to point B in order to do what needs to be done at point B as soon as possible so that you can move on to point C. There is no point in a leisurely walk.

- Slow down! Try to focus your senses to notice what is going on around you. The smell of spring, cute squirrels playing tag, a cool breeze... whatever it is that makes you happy.
- "It isn't about the breaths you take, but the moments that take your breath away."
- There will always be more stuff on your to do list. Realistically, in what ways will slowing down cause you harm?

To overcome this time-management style, first look for the motivation behind your behavior.

- Why do you have to be "superhuman" or "perfect?"

Often, you are either seeking approval or running from some other source of anxiety or frustration.

- From whom are you trying to get approval?
- What happens if you are compassionate with yourself and approve of yourself, imperfections and all?

The next step is to begin dealing with the fears/anxiety underlying the hostility. If you are not perfect, the most efficient, always in control or always doing something "purposeful," how could that lead to...

- Rejection? How can you deal with that?
- Failure? How can you deal with that?
- The unknown/loss of control? How can you deal with that?

Activity: Time Juggler

If you are a time juggler, you do as many things at one time as you possibly can. For instance, shaving and driving to work while talking on the hands-free car phone. Time jugglers are often quite successful at accomplishing the small tasks, but have difficulty producing quality output in complex things. Multi-tasking in itself is not a problem. It is only when time juggling starts to impair the quality of your work or begins causing undue emotional stress that it is a problem.

Again, the question arises: Why do you have to do so much in such a short time? Are you a poor time manager? Do you procrastinate? Do you underestimate the time it will take, or forget about things like travel, lunch and the all-important coffee break? If this sounds like you, practice making lists and prioritizing.

You may also end up doing too much because you cannot say "no." This may indicate that you have low self-esteem and are afraid of being rejected if you do not always comply. Learning how to manage your time, set boundaries so you don't feel guilty for not always being there for everyone else and assertively say "no" are priorities for you.

You may also have too much to do because you create a situation where multi-tasking is inevitable. This gives you have an excuse if everything does not turn out right. This is called "self-handicapping." It is a method of preserving self-esteem when you fear you may fail. You expect that, if people see how much you had going on, they will not see failure as a negative reflection on your abilities.

- Since Time Jugglers can often accomplish simple tasks effectively, if you have a complex task at hand, break it into small, manageable, independent parts.

- Learn how to set boundaries, say "no."

- Eliminate unnecessary tasks, delegate those that do not require your specific attention and prioritize the ones that are left.

- Finally, if time juggling is the result of self-handicapping, address your fears of failure, ask for help and try to devote as much undivided time to it as possible. In the end, your self-esteem will benefit because you will have accomplished a task you did not think you could.

Activity: Procrastinator

If you are a procrastinator, you either knowingly or unknowingly do something other than the task that needs completion. You knowingly accomplish this by saying things like "I'll do it tomorrow." Unknowingly you may accomplish this by starting the task but then slipping into superfluous things such as "getting organized" so you can more efficiently do the task. I can spend an entire day organizing my office, so I can "be more efficient at writing my notes." In reality, I am just avoiding the inevitable. Procrastination can be addressed by looking at the reasons for not doing (or completing) a task, such as fear or failure, boredom, dread, apathy. . .

Why do you procrastinate? To self-handicap so you can use the excuse that you did not have enough time? Because you are overwhelmed with too many things at once, or a task which seems insurmountable? Because you dislike what you have to do, and/or there are 100 other things you would rather do?

Addressing Procrastination. So how can procrastination be overcome?

- Acknowledge your feelings about the task.

- Combine it with something you do like or make engaging in a favorite activity contingent upon completing the task or a measurable portion of the task.

- Identify all of the ways in which you procrastinate (I clean and lose track of time in my garden).

- Get a supportive person to encourage you and make sure you stay on task.

- Break tasks into smaller components and have rewards after each segment.

- Plan ahead for foreseeable stressors on which you may procrastinate and eliminate as many other stressors as possible. For instance, do your shopping and packing before finals, so you can concentrate on studying for finals and truly enjoying time not spent studying.

- Make lists of everything which needs to be done.

  - Prioritize: divide your lists into "must dos" and "would like to do."
  - Delegate any tasks that someone else could do

- Eliminate clutter (Your environment usually represents how you feel on the inside)

- Set aside one day to pay the bills, cook for the week, or run errands

- Try and accomplish multiple simple tasks at the same time, for instance making telephone calls and folding the laundry, or unloading the dishwasher while you are waiting for something to cook

- Make sure other areas of your life are not placing undue stress and hampering your productivity (i.e. a significant other who is upset because you have not paid enough attention to him/her)

Activity: Perfectionist

If you are a perfectionist, you spend too much time trying to make whatever it is perfect. The end product is never good enough. By wasting time on the illusion of perfection, you prevent yourself from accomplishing other activities. You may need to evaluate what you are trying to gain by achieving the unachievable.

You may have had conditions of worth placed on you for what you do; therefore, to feel good enough, what you do must be perfect. Or, you may be plagued with the "imposter phenomenon," and believe you are not very good at anything and, despite your achievements, you constantly fear someone finding out how incompetent you believe you truly are. You rarely believe your work is good enough and constantly strive to make it better even though you are doing much more than anyone else.

If you are a perfectionist, you need to evaluate how you are spending your energy. Often you will see you are devoting almost all of your time and energy to "perfecting" things that will, in five years from now, mean nothing. Is it worth sacrificing an evening out with your friends to revise your work three more times to get an A+ instead of an A? Or spending an extra 2 hours dusting the blinds, door frames and windowsills before your mother comes over? There comes a point of diminishing returns when you are investing a significant amount of energy for very minor improvements.

Perfectionists always need to keep in mind three questions:

- Is this worth ignoring all of the other things in my life?
- Will this matter a year from now?
- How much difference will it make to get it 1% better?

Activity: Eager to Please

The eager to please style is closely related to the time juggler. If you are eager to please, you cannot say "no." You become so bogged down in helping everyone do everything that you can hardly keep sight of yourself. If you are eager to please, you need to work on developing personal boundaries and respecting those boundaries. What would happen if you told someone "no"?

If you are genuinely driven by a desire to help others and are a poor time manager who just loses sight of the number of commitments you make, you can benefit by _never agreeing to anything on the spot._ Take time out to think about whether you have the time to take on something else. If the task is something you feel very strongly about doing, then before you agree to it you need to eliminate or delay other commitments to make time.

Keep a log of all of your commitments--including those constant day-to-day things like work, school, spending time with significant others and exercise. This will help you be able to identify how to use your energy to help you move toward what is important and set boundaries with less guilt.

Finally, if you really do not have time to do it or it is something that you do not really want to do, but you feel obligated to say "yes," ask yourself:

- Why do I feel I need to agree to this?
- What will (realistically) happen if I say no?

General Suggestions. Time is constant, irreversible and irreplaceable. It needs to be effectively managed to be effective. Analyze how you spend your time and implement a few time saving methods that will gain you the most time. The following are examples of some of the biggest time wasters:

- Indecision
- Interruptions
- Procrastination
- Unrealistic time estimates
- Unnecessary errors
- Delegating tasks without clearly stating your expectations

Activity: Eliminate, Delegate and Prioritize

Make a list of everything you "need" to do

Review the list and cross off anything that does not HAVE TO be done (Have to's are things like: paying bills etc. in which there will be a big problem if you don't do them).

Now, identify any that can be delegated to a spouse, child or co-worker

With what is left, prioritize and simplify what needs to be done first. Remember that getting things done is sometimes a matter of degree. When you are busy, cooking a 5-course meal from scratch can be replaced by a simpler meal, or one you pick up from a local deli.

Goal Setting

Once you have decided to make a positive change and the commitment is clear, goals should be set. Goal setting is part of exploring your new life and figuring out what you want and like to do. Set realistic, specific goals in multiple areas of your life. Talk with others and learn why your prior attempts to achieve goals have failed so you don't make the same mistake again. Initially, goals should be short-term, measurable and realistic. Focus on one or two.

Before committing to long-term change, you may benefit from experimenting with a short period. Try out your new behavior for a week. Keep a journal of how it felt, and what goals may need to be modified because it was too hard or unpleasant. Sometimes it is a matter of slowing the process. For example, instead of starting to eat healthier by totally changing your diet, start by only having sugary foods once a day, then reduce it to once a week. Once you are comfortable with that then try, for example, carrying a water bottle with you to help you drink more water.

You need to be aware of the reasons you want to change (or not), how motivated you are to change different aspects of your life, how to increase your motivation levels and how to make changes in a way that works for you. Yes, that's right. One size does not fit all. Remember, Rome was not built in a day, and neither were your problems. However, everything is intertwined. That is the good news. Positive changes in one area will have positive changes on other areas. Break large goals down into smaller ones that can be accomplished a week at a time. Go through the questions below. Pick one or two things to work on and see how positive changes in one area cause positive changes in the rest of your life.

Activity: Experimenting with Change.

Answer the following questions for one or two goals, and then, get started!

1. The change I want to make is…Be specific. Include goals that are positive (wanting to increase, improve, do more of something), and not just negative goals (stop, avoid, or decrease a behavior).

2. My main reasons for making this change are…

3. What are the likely consequences of action or inaction?

4. Which motivations for change are most compelling?

5. The first steps I plan to take in changing are…

6. When, where, and how will the steps be taken?

7. Some things that could interfere with my plan are…

8. How will I stick with the plan despite these particular problems or setbacks?

9. Other people could help me in changing in these ways…

10. I will know that my plan is working when…

Physical

You have learned about your basic emotions and are becoming aware of what makes you tick. Now you are going to learn about physical interventions. There are a myriad of reasons why physical interventions are so helpful in treating depression and anxiety.

- They release endorphins, serotonin, dopamine and norepinephrine (all happy chemicals)
- They increase the available oxygen in your blood which helps with confusion and "foggy head."
- They have been linked to improvements in self-esteem
- They help you get your mind/thoughts and bodily reactions more in synch.
- They often put you in a place where you can engage with other positive people
- They can help with general aches and pains which can disrupt your sleep and put you in a bad mood.
- They can help you turn down the stress response, so you sleep better
- They can help increase your energy

Prior to making changes in your physical activity or nutrition, it is advisable to see your doctor. During that visit, you can be assessed for thyroid or hormone imbalances as well as vitamin D deficiency which have all been linked to feelings of depression and anxiety.

Yoga

Yoga's unique mind-body approach is being used more and more to reduce stress, treat depression, and enhance overall well-being. The following three studies provide some insight into the benefits of yoga for depression and anxiety:

One study reported that your calming brain chemical, GABA, increases after a session of yoga. (J Alternative and Complementary Medicine, 2007).

In another study in the Medical Science Monitor (2005) found that women who were suffering from mental distress, showed "significant improvements on measures of stress and psychological outcomes" after participating in a three-month yoga class.

In a third study, thirteen psychiatric inpatients were studied to determine the effects of yoga on mood. Participants reported significant improvements in tension-anxiety, depression-dejection, anger-hostility, fatigue-inertia, and confusion-bewilderment. (Psychiatric Rehabilitation Journal, Spring 2005).

Yoga can be a powerful practice for depression or anxiety, and a key component of this is the breath. The breathing used in yoga can help calm your stress response system and contribute to a state of relaxation. The result is a mind-body connection that can have far-reaching effects. In the meantime, try this simple exercise.

Activity: Grounding Activity

1. Go to a comfortable place. Turn off your cell phone. Put a do-not disturb sign on your door and put the dogs somewhere that you will not scare the snot out of you if the UPS man comes.

2. Sit down and lean back, of just lay down (Initially this is hard to do when you are sitting straight up.)

3. Breathe in through your nose for a count of four, inflating your stomach like a balloon. (Most Americans chest breathe which is very shallow and inefficient). Hold your breath for a count of 4 and exhale for a count of 4.

4. With each exhale, feel the stress leaving your body.

5. By slowing your breathing, you are cuing your heart that it is time to relax and slow down. This can reduce the stress response and purge the adrenaline so you feel less like the squirrel in the road.

Meditation

Meditation does help manage anxiety, depression and pain, but does not appear to help with other problems according to the 47 studies analyzed in an article published in *JAMA Internal Medicine, 2014.*

Dr. Madhav Goyal, of Johns Hopkins School of Medicine says the positive effects of meditation on anxiety, depression and pain can be modest, but are seen across multiple studies, and about 2.5 hours of meditation practice per week (20-30 minutes per day) produces consistent effects.

Guided meditations are literally recordings of someone who verbally talks you through a meditation session. There are a variety of guided meditations geared toward managing depression and/or anxiety that are freely available on the internet (YouTube). If you have anxiety or difficulty clearing your mind, start with guided imagery meditations because they give you something to focus on besides clearing your head.

Additionally, don't let the thought of meditating the "right" way add to your stress. You can make meditation as formal or informal as you like, however it suits your lifestyle and situation. Some people build meditation into their daily routine. For example, you may start and end each day with a half hour of meditation. All you really *need* is a few minutes of quiet time.

I meditate when I run by focusing on the rhythmic foot strikes. I also meditate when I am weeding in the garden. All I am thinking about is the plot of ground right in front of me, clearing my mind of all the other noise.

Activity: Meditation Practice

Here are examples of ways to practice meditation on your own, whenever you choose. Pick one and try doing it for a week 20 minutes a day.

- Breathe deeply. This technique is good for beginners because breathing is a natural function.

- Focused breathing. Concentrate on feeling and listening as you inhale and exhale through your nostrils. Breathe deeply and slowly. When your attention wanders, gently return your focus to your breathing.

- Body Scan. When using this technique, focus attention on different parts of your body. Become aware of your body's various sensations, whether that's pain, tension, warmth or relaxation. Focus on trying to relax any areas that are tense.

- Focused attention. Focus all of your attention on one thing, like a candle flame or a swimming goldfish.

- Open monitoring. Instead of focusing on any one object, you keep your attention open to whatever presents itself. The easiest way to try this is to go outside and watch the sky, a babbling brook or the ocean.

- Repeat a mantra. You can create your own mantra, whether it's religious or secular. "I am awesome." "It is what it is" "Relax" or whatever other message you want to send to yourself.

- My personal favorite is mindfulness meditation which I do when trail running. Mindfulness meditation is the practice of intentionally focusing on the present moment, accepting and non-judgmentally paying attention to the sensations, thoughts, and emotions that arise. I am aware of what I see so I don't fall, my breathing, the joy it brings me when I see a woodland creature, how good the cool breeze feels, etc. My mind stays occupied so I am unable to dwell on all of the stresses, anxieties, frustrations and obsessions I may have.

- Engage in prayer. Prayer is the best known and most widely practiced example of meditation. Spoken and written prayers are found in most faith traditions. The Catholic Rosary or the Stations of the Cross are good examples of prayer-based meditation.

- Read and reflect. Many people report that they benefit from reading poems or sacred texts, and taking a few moments to quietly reflect on their meaning.

- You can also listen to music, you find relaxing or inspiring. You may want to write your reflections in a journal or discuss you with a friend or spiritual leader.

- Focus on a painting. I personally like Thomas Kinkade for the warm, country scenes, but whatever works for you. Imagine yourself in the painting. What does it feel like? What does it smell like? What do you hear?

- Loving Kindness Meditation. Focus your attention on generating in your heart and mind feelings of compassion and acceptance for the following people, one at a time:
  - Oneself
  - A good friend
  - A "neutral" person
  - A difficult person
  - All four of the above equally
  - And then gradually the entire universe

Don't judge yourself, which may only increase your stress and depression. Meditation takes practice. It's common for your mind to wander during meditation, no matter how long you've been practicing it. If you're meditating to calm your mind and your attention wanders, simply return to the object, sensation or movement you're focusing on. That's it. No judgement.

Experiment, and you'll likely find out what types of meditation work best for you and what you enjoy doing. Other types of meditation can be found at: https://liveanddare.com/types-of-meditation

Exercise

When most people hear the word exercise, they groan. Most of your life you have probably been taught that exercise means weight lifting, taking aerobics classes or doing something else equally as dreadful. While some of us may thrive on that, the vast majority of people would rather do just about anything than go to the gym. If you are one of those people, don't despair. Exercise can help you get your body moving and increase serotonin and oxygen in your bloodstream which can help relieve aches and pains, feelings of fatigue (sounds weird I know), and depression. Exercise is anything that gets your body moving.

Activity: Get Moving

Make a list of things you like to do that involve movement and post it somewhere conspicuous. (Yes, sex can be on the list, so can cleaning house or washing your car). All of these are exercise. Will they make you into an Olympic athlete or an NFL football player, probably not, but that is not your goal. Your goal is to balance your muscles, increase the oxygen in your bloodstream and get that heart rate above couch-potato level. It is important to be kind to yourself, especially if you have not exercised in a while. Set a goal to do 20 minutes of some type of exercise each day.

Activity: Make Exercise Fun

Identify 10 ways you can make the exercises you identified more tolerable. Here are a few suggestions. Do it with a friend. Exercise by walking through the mall (Some malls even open early for walkers). Play hide and seek with your kids. Take your dog on a walk. Allow yourself to sit in the hot-tub afterward. Make it a competition. Watch television on your ipad while you walk on the treadmill. Inflate balloons and keep them from touching the ground (Your kids and animals will want to get in on the fun!). Listen to your favorite music while exercising (or even your favorite comedian).

Activity: Stretch

Stretch each morning and evening—just 5 minutes, and whenever you start feeling "tense" during the day. When your muscles are not twingey and out-of-whack, it is easier to concentrate, less tiring to do things and you will sleep better, thus improving your mood.

Relaxation

All work and no play makes Jack a dull boy is true for everyone, not just Jack Nicholson. Relaxation techniques do nothing to change or block feelings about events, but you can help clear your mind and find your "center." It is a time-out for the entire body. Relaxation techniques are also used to help you identify and eliminate sources of wasted energy in your life. That is, when you feel like you are going in a million different directions, you may be less efficient about making decisions or accomplishing tasks. This can lead to feelings of frustration with yourself which compounds depression. Further, if you are physically tense, you are wasting energy to maintain that muscle tension, and causing yourself some level of pain, which again, negatively impacts your mood.

Below are a few techniques you can use to relax.

Activity: Try Reflexology or Massage

Reflexology is an ancient healing art based upon the premise that, by massaging certain pressure points, you can relieve energy blocks, or deposits and thus reduce distress. However, the current scheme linking various parts of the foot with specific parts of the body got its start in the early 1900's, by Dr. William H. Fitzgerald. In the 1930's, Eunice Ingham, a nurse and physiotherapist refined the system, identifying especially sensitive areas she called "reflex points" and creating a map of the body as represented on the feet. There are also corresponding points on the hands and ears. You can find videos online to help you work these points or see a reflexologist or massage therapist.

Activity: Cued Progressive Muscular Relaxation

Do you remember when you were in school and two words could strike fear into everyone in the class— "Pop quiz." That is an example of a cue. If you say "pop quiz" to a 5 year old, he will have no idea what you are talking about. Over time, the word pop quiz became linked with anxiety for you. Eventually, you did not even need to see the quiz, someone just had to say the words. Okay, so how does this apply? Instead of a word or phrase making you anxious, Cued Progressive Muscular Relaxation teaches you to associate a word with the relaxation response. For me it is "breathe" (partly because when I get stressed I forget to breathe, so it was a logical word to choose). With each exhale, I say to myself "breathe" and feel my muscles relax. I do this several times when I lay down at night to help myself relax and get to sleep. Sport Psychology for Coaches by Damon Burton, Thomas D. Raedeke has a good chapter on relaxation. You can also just search the internet for "cued progressive muscular relaxation script."

Activity: Exercise The Other Part Of Your Brain

I do relatively creative things all day long. At night, I give that side of my brain a rest and switch over to logic puzzles. Unblock Me, Words with Friends, Checkers and Minesweeper are my favorite. I get into a totally different zone. What are 5 things you can do to exercise the alternate side of your brain? If you are logical all day (Accountant, scientist etc.) try doing something creative. If you are creative (teacher, artist, chef) try doing something more analytical.

Activity: Exploring Your Hobbies and Interests

When you become depressed, hobbies and recreational activities are often the first to go. This is a travesty. These are often the things that bring happiness into your life. So many of my patients do not even know what makes them happy anymore. Hobbies are great for healing depression because they give you a sense of accomplishment; make you happy, and often connect you with positive people with similar interests.

1. Make a list of things you like to do (baking, drawing, ham radio, fishing, exercising, gardening, shooting, photography... the list is endless)

2. Start scheduling a time each week to do your hobby/hobbies. You may find that you can do them at the same time you are doing other things. I love to crochet, but hate  to travel (or sit still for that matter). Whenever we go anywhere, I always bring my crochet. (TSA will still allow crochet hooks on the plane, but not knitting needles...lol.) Now that I have more scarves that a woman could possibly wear, I have started crocheting wraps for the homeless. This has led me to develop a sewing circle in my community. We all share our talents and ideas.

3. Take a community class. Maybe you will find a hobby you never dreamed you would like.

4. Get a buddy. There will be days that you feel too guilty to take time for your hobby. A buddy will remind you that you deserve to take an hour or two for yourself.

Hobbies and recreation are important ways for you to clear your mind, get rejuvenated and "sharpen the saw." They also help you connect with other like-minded people for fun and social support, all of which help relieve depression.

Nutrition

You can practice meditation, relaxation, hobbies, positive thinking all day long, but if your body doesn't have the building blocks to make the brain chemicals that help you feel motivated, happy, and, yes, even stressed, you are not going to be as happy as you could be. It gets these building blocks from good healthy food. (As a side note, taking vitamins is not a replacement for a healthy diet.) Some biological causes of depression can be linked to poor nutrition which keeps the body from being able to make the brain chemicals to support your mood.

Serotonin is a brain chemical made from the amino acid (protein) L-Tryptophan. It regulates sleep, calms you down and assists with pain regulation. Melatonin is made from serotonin and is a hormone that controls your sleep cycle. They are totally interrelated. During the evening, the body's serotonin levels rise and melatonin is created and released to start the natural sleep cycle. If you don't have enough serotonin, this will affect the production of melatonin and you will not sleep well. Low serotonin is one of the reasons people with depression do not ever feel rested and have low energy.

Foods with serotonin boosting power provide L-tryptophan and vitamin B6. L-Tryptophan is found in foods like cottage cheese, brown rice, avocados, **bananas**, **walnuts**, **tomatoes**, **sunflower or sesame seeds,** soy protein, dark **chicken and turkey meat**, and starchy carbohydrates (bread, pasta, carrots and potatoes). B6 can be found in **sunflower or sesame seeds**, **turkey or chicken**, **bananas,** prunes (plums), and **avocadoes**. (Note: The foods in bold provide both L-Tryptophan and B6). It is not hard to incorporate some of these into your meals. Try adding 2 tablespoons of crushed walnuts and a sliced banana to your cereal or oatmeal each morning (or just pack whole ones for a convenient snack).

As an aside, end-stage renal diseases, chronic renal insufficiency, and other kidney diseases as well as malabsorption syndromes, such as celiac disease, Crohn's disease, and ulcerative colitis can cause vitamin B6 deficiency. If you have any of these concerns, of course, consult your physician. Without B6 your body cannot efficiently make serotonin.

Your body naturally wants to create the optimum balance of neurotransmitters to help you feel happy, alert and be able to respond to threats. How can you get that balance? Make your body as healthy as possible, reduce unnecessary stress, eat a good diet, and do enjoyable things that will increase dopamine, serotonin and norepinephrine levels. You can also see your doctor about medication, but medication cannot fix nutritional deficiencies.

Activity: Create a Menu

It is easy to eat the first thing you see if you don't have a plan. Make a menu for at least a week at a time to guide your shopping. That way, when you are hungry you aren't trying to remember all the principles of healthy eating like having three colors on your plate at each meal.

Remember that taking various vitamins as supplements often does not provide them in the best ratio for your body to use them and can even do more harm than good. It is much easier for your body to use nutrients from healthy foods. Below is a sample list to consider.

- 5 types of vegetables: Broccoli, peas, carrots, spinach, celery
- 3 fruits: Tomato paste, diced tomatoes, spaghetti sauce, bananas, apples
- Brown rice
- Oatmeal
- Pasta (whole wheat)
- Bread (whole wheat)
- Lentils
- Meat: Turkey, tuna, pork loin
- American cheese slices
- Walnut pieces
- Sunflower seeds
- Sugar free drink mix
- Caffeine free black or green tea
- Milk
- Cottage cheese
- Taco seasoning
- Healthy cereal
- Eggs

Sample meals

Breakfasts

- Cereal or oatmeal with sliced peaches, blueberries, raisins, or strawberries
- Eggs, cantaloupe or pineapple and whole grain toast
- Cottage cheese and fruit with walnuts or almonds
- Pancakes with pureed fruit topping and milk
- Apple cinnamon pancakes
- Low fat zucchini or carrot pancakes (like low fat zucchini bread or carrot cake but cooked like a pancake)
- Peanut butter, banana and raisin sandwich
- Homemade trail mix with almonds, raisins, crasins, walnuts and steel-cut oats
- Apple salad with red and green apples, walnuts and rasins

Lunches and Dinners

- Spaghetti or lasagne with primavera sauce that includes diced red and green peppers, zucchini, carrots and broccoli. I will even throw finely diced kale in as well.
- Grilled cheese with green peas or tomato soup
- Supreme or veggie lovers pizza
- Meat loaf or lentil loaf with green beans, carrots, peas and tomato paste
- Tacos or taco salad with cheese, lettuce or spinach and salsa
- Shepherd's pie
- Vegetable soup (with chicken or beef if you want meat)
- Low fat quiche
- Chili with black beans and corn served over a bed of lettuce or spinach
- Black beans and brown rice with broccoli
- Chicken, rice, cheese and broccoli bake
- Tuna casserole (can substitute salmon for a boost of omega 3s)
- Vegetable stir fry with sesame seeds. Add chicken or beef if you like. (This makes a good side-dish too)

Other Nutritional Interventions

- Saffron is a well-known Persian spice used for its ability to help the digestive system heal. As the most expensive spice, it is high in carotenoids and B vitamins. In studies, saffron has been compared to both Prozac and Imipramine, and found to work at least as well, or better, with less side effects.

- Cherry tomato skin is rich in lycopene, a phytonutrient that actually stops the build-up of pro-inflammatory compounds linked to depression. Because lycopene lives in tomato skins, the best way to get it is through cherry tomatoes.

- Black-eyed peas have some of the highest levels of folate of any vegetable. Folate plays a role in creating dopamine, serotonin, and norepinephrine, three brain chemicals that, when absent, can make you forgetful, irritable, and unable to sleep.

- Oregano is rich in caffeic acid, quercetin, and rosmarinic acid, all components that combat depression, fatigue, and anxiety. (Oh, and it is really easy to grow!)

- Sunflower seeds are a great source for the antidepressant phenylalanine, an amino acid the body turns into norepinephrine.

- Water. Don't. Forget. Water. Dehydration will leave you feeling sluggish, fatigued and depressed.

As an aside, some research has identified selenium, copper and zinc as crucial in the fight against aging. Guess what, these are also found in brown rice, bananas, spinach, turkey, chicken, cottage cheese, walnuts, and sesame and sunflower seeds, so you are getting mood boosting and anti-ageing properties.

Sleep

Sleep is the time your body gets to repair. It is able to divert all that energy you usually spend on moving, talking, thinking, fretting, stewing, and even digesting on repairing and rebalancing. Your body is fascinating in that it naturally seeks balance. When you go on a strict diet, your body slows your metabolism because it thinks there is a famine. When you eat  too much salt, it retains water to keep the fluid/salt balance regulated. After you have the flu, it also stores fluid, in response to recovering from dehydration. Everything it does is often explainable in terms of trying to maintain a balance.

If your sleep is inadequate, or poor, then it does not have time to do its work. This leads to a much more inefficient system. Look at presidents over the course of your terms. They age very rapidly. Part of this is stress, but part is lack of adequate, quality sleep. Their bodies cannot deal with all of the stress, keep them healthy, and repair damaged tissue without having some "down-time." Think about when you are tired. Your body is trying to finish up what it would have when you were sleeping while you are trying to concentrate, make decisions, remember what your co-worker just said and who knows what else. Being overwhelmed, "foggy headed" and lacking energy, are all symptoms of a lack of quality sleep and depression and can compound any existing feelings of helplessness.

Activity: Tips for Improving Sleep

Create a plan using the tips below to improve your sleep.

- Keep work and bills out of the bedroom
- Eliminate as much light as possible (Sleep masks help)
- Turn on an air purifier for "white noise"
- Wear comfortable clothing that breathes like 100% cotton
- Use aromatherapy scents on your pillows or in a diffuser (lavender, chamomile, catnip, valerian)
- Keep a pad and pen and a RED light by your bed in case you think of something--you can write it down, so you do not worry about forgetting it.
- Do not exercise or eat a heavy meal within 3 hours of going to bed
- Eliminate caffeine within 8 hours of bedtime.
- Try to go to bed at the same time each night
- Create a bedtime routine. Just like your kids (dinner, bath, story, bed), if you have the same routine each night, your body will start cuing in and secreting melatonin sooner. I eat dinner, brush my teeth, get changed, and play a logic game on my tablet.

- If you must nap, limit it to 40 minutes so you do not enter into a REM sleep cycle.

- If it takes more than 15 minutes to get to sleep, get up and do something for 30 minutes then try again. Otherwise you may lay in bed and get frustrated that you cannot sleep, which will keep you awake!

Sunlight

Ahhh, the benefits of sunlight for depression. There are two main benefits of sunlight— creation of vitamin D and synching your circadian rhythms.

Vitamin D helps with immune system, muscle, and cardiovascular function, for a healthy body. Additionally, some of the receptors in the areas of your brain that are linked to the development of depression are receptors for vitamin D. For this reason, vitamin D deficiency has been linked with depression and with other mental health problems. Exactly how vitamin D works in your brain isn't fully understood. Researchers have suggested that vitamin D may increase the amount of "happy" chemicals, which has an effect on depression.

It is important to note that vitamin D that your body synthesizes from the sun is far more effective and available than the synthetic supplements that you take. That does not mean you should suddenly start slathering on the baby oil and going to the beach again. However, getting a little sun either before 10am or after 4pm could be hugely beneficial to your health and mood.

Your circadian rhythms tell your body when it is time to be awake and when it is time to wind down and control those pesky hormones like melatonin (your sleep hormone). Circadian rhythms are partly cued by light levels. When it is bright, your brain thinks it is time to be awake, so it will not release melatonin. This is why it is recommended for night shift workers to end their shift and get in bed before sunrise. This is also why it is harder to sleep in a bright room. When it is dark, your brain thinks it is time for sleep and will make you more relaxed and sleepier. When you are depressed, you may tend to stay in a dark room which will keep you feeling like you cannot wake up and are exhausted all the time. This can be a signal that you are not getting quality sleep, and/or your circadian rhythms are out of whack.

One of the easiest interventions for depression that I have used (very successfully) with many of my patients is what I call—"Rise and sunshine." Many people with depression have gotten their circadian (sleep/wake) rhythms out of whack. When they do sleep, it is not quality. When they are awake, they are always sleepy. Sound familiar?

Activity: Rise and Sunshine

Try to start getting up at a reasonable hour for you and sit by a sunny window while you eat your breakfast. Throughout the day, go outside just to remind your body that it is still daytime. If you are not working, still get up, get dressed, sit by a sunny window or on your porch. In the evening, go through your sleep routine and shut out as much light as possible. It will take time, but your body will cue into the new schedule. During the winter when the days are shorter, and it is dark when you go to work and dark when you are leaving work, it is even more important to keep it bright during the day, and dim at night.

Pain Management

Everyone experiences aches and pains. Expecting to never feel pain is not realistic. However, when you are depressed, you may be feeling more pain. Serotonin levels are not only responsible (in part) for your mood and sleep, but also for your perception of pain. When you have low serotonin levels, you may tend to perceive more pain than when you have adequate serotonin. Additionally, if you have something like colitis or Chron's disease, you may be more susceptible to low serotonin levels. Check out with your doctor.

Pain can provoke feelings like anxiety, irritability, and agitation in anyone. All these are normal feelings when you are hurting. Normally, as pain subsides, so do the unpleasant feelings. But what if the pain doesn't go away? Over time, the constantly activated stress response can cause multiple problems associated with depression. Those problems can include sleep disturbances, difficulty concentrating, fatigue, irritability, grief or frustration over the limitations caused by the pain, and reduced activity. The end result can often be summed up as "depression." Once depression sets in, it magnifies the pain that is already there. So what can you do?

Activity: Pain Management

- Pay attention to ergonomics. The way you are sitting, standing and sleeping has a huge impact on potential muscle aches and pains. For example, I often sit sideways on the couch with my legs pulled up under me. This causes one shoulder to be much higher than the other and my spine to be out of whack. The same is true when I work on the computer. My shoulder on my mousing arm is often higher than my other one. Both of these contribute to my neck and shoulder pain. By practicing good posture much of my muscle pain can be reduced.
    - If you don't wake up feeling rested/energized, look into sleeping ergonomics. Your spine needs to be properly aligned for the best sleep and pain prevention.
    - Make sure your workstation is ergonomically sound. Learn more at the Occupational Health and Safety Administration's website. https://www.osha.gov/SLTC/ergonomics/
    - Do you have a baby on your hip half the day? Try to find ways, like a baby bjorn, to carry your bundle of joy in a more centered position, or at least alternate hips.
    - If you carry a purse or computer bag (especially a heavy one) try to get one with a strap that goes across your body, or alternate which shoulder you carry it on. Shoulder packs often cause you to raise your shoulder a bit to keep them in place.

- Stretch. Remember that your body wants to remain balanced. If one side is all tensed up, the other side will be fighting it. Stretch, especially your neck, upper back and hamstrings. As an aside, did you know that tight chest muscles can actually cause numbness in your hands that can be mistaken for carpal tunnel? If you do not know what to do, there are plenty of YouTube videos that can walk you through it.   Of course, get a doctor's approval before changing any physical activity.

- Talk with your doctor about TENS units, massage, hydrotherapy, hypnosis or other non-narcotic interventions. (Narcotics are depressants and highly addictive, so they are not the preferred intervention)

Medication

Have you ever listened to a commercial for a medication and the side effects sound far worse than the condition itself? Medication can be helpful, but it also can cause problems. Part of dealing with your depression is to understand what each medication does, if it helps more than it hurts and what your options are. Evaluate the medications you are taking and talk with your doctor. Some medications you are taking for your mood, blood pressure, pain or anything else may be contributing to your depression.

Additionally, medications often do not cure the underlying problem in your brain chemical balance. Taking medication to address depression is like turning up water pressure to address a leaky pipe. Yes, it gets things back to normal for the time being, but doesn't address the underlying issue. Antidepressants can be a great help to people with depression or anxiety to give them a jump start on feeling better while their body is recovering, they are finding the causes of their neurochemical imbalanced and developing tools to address the problem. Many people, however, are able to discontinue those medications after a period. (Always consult your doctor before starting or stopping any medication).

Antidepressants

These medications can be helpful with depression and anxiety for about 35% of the population. What you may not know is that each antidepressant works slightly differently---even the ones in the same family. For example, Zoloft, Paxil and Prozac all have very valid uses, but all affect you quite differently. Zoloft tends to be pretty neutral in that it helps with anxiety and depression, but doesn't tend to rev people up or make them super sleepy. Patients who take Paxil often report it makes them sleepy. This can be overcome by taking the dose at night. Patients taking Prozac often report an increase in energy and/or anxiety. These reactions are not true for everyone, but it is important to know what you may experience when starting medications.

There are dozens of antidepressants out there. I am not going to go into all of them here. The important point is to know that there probably is one that will work better than others for you. The key is to talk with your doctor and do your own research. Drugs.com has forums where patients can post their experiences on different medications.

Antianxiety (Benzodiazepines)

Depression can be caused by being anxious and feeling helpless for too long. The most common antianxiety medications are things like Xanax and Valium. They are sometimes used to treat not only anxiety, but also muscle pain. The biggest draw backs to benzodiazepines are the high potential for abuse, the connection between long term use and developing dementia and the potentially life threatening withdrawal. All of those things aside, it is important to understand that there are three main types of benzodiazapines. The first type, short acting, get into your system quickly, provide relief and exit quickly. These tend to be more problematic for people with depression and/or anxiety because the crash is so sudden. The second type is intermediate acting. These drugs also get into your system quickly, but exit more slowly so the change is not so dramatic. The third, of course is the long acting. Valium and Librium both fall into this category. If you and your physician decide that benzodiazepines are a good choice for you, I encourage you to consider the longer acting to reduce the jolts on your system.

Pain Killers (Opiates)

Not all pain relievers are opiates, but that is what I am going to focus on here. Opiates (hydrocodone, oxycodone, fentanyl etc) do help reduce your pain, but you are also depressants. The can cause fatigue, difficulty concentrating, constipation, and changes in sleeping and eating patterns. These side-effects are also symptoms of depression. It is also notable that opiates can have negative interactions with some antidepressants, antianxiety medications and antihistamines (like Benadryl). Since opiates slow your system, combining them with antianxiety medications or antihistamines which also slow your system can cause respiratory distress among other problems.

Activity: Medications

- Examine the medications you are taking. Do any of them have side effects that are contributing to your depression, sleep problems or difficulty concentrating? Do not discontinue medication without talking to your doctor, but if you find that depression might be a side effect of certain medications, do talk to your doctor.
- What issues do you currently have that might benefit from medication or other interventions? (Sleep problems, anxiety, depression, chronic pain…)

Please remember the key question to ask (and keep asking) is "What is keeping my brain chemicals out of whack?" Negative thoughts, pain, certain medications, poor nutrition, too much caffeine, addictive behaviors, inadequate quality sleep, trauma, thyroid or sex hormone imbalances, "stress" can all cause neurochemical imbalances. Taking an antidepressant doesn't eliminate the causes of the imbalance, it simply seeks to artificially rebalance it. Unfortunately, like you have learned, it is very difficulty to know if your depression is caused by too little serotonin, norepinephrine, glutamate or dopamine. Further, there are multiple types of serotonin and norepinephrine receptors which all respond to different antidepressants.

The take home messages:

- If you decide to try medications it is certainly possible they can help, especially in the short term, but it might take trying a few different medications to find the one that works for you.

- Mental health medications can only do so much. To truly get better, you need to be willing to address at least some of the lifestyle factors and thinking patterns that are keeping your neurotransmitters out of whack.

Social

Researchers have found that your relationships can be one of the greatest buffers against stress, and depression. Friends can listen to you rant, provide alternate perspectives, validate your thoughts, feelings and reactions and generally just help you feel less isolated.

The key, obviously, is finding, developing and maintaining healthy relationships. If you are in a relationship with someone who is depressed, or if your relationship is faltering, that can cause or increase your depression. Relationships with a depressed partner are often characterized by negative communication, blame, withdrawal, irritability, loss of motivation, and loss of sexual interest for both parties. It has also been shown that when one partner is depressed, there is a reduction in positive behavior such as eye contact, smiling, and the ability to enjoy pleasurable activities together.

A strong social support network can be critical to help you through the stress of tough times, whether you've had a bad day at work or a year filled with loss or chronic illness. Since your supportive family, friends, and co-workers are such an important part of your life, it's never too soon to cultivate these important relationships. (Notice I said "supportive." Who is it that you want in your life that provides support and brings out the best in you?)

What is a social support network?

A social support network is made up of friends, family and peers. A social support network is different from a support group, which is generally a structured meeting run by a mental health professional. Although both can play an important role in times of stress, a social support network is something you can develop when you're not under stress. It provides the comfort of knowing that you have friends there for you if you need them.

Benefits of a social support network

Numerous studies have demonstrated that having a network of supportive relationships contributes to psychological well-being. When you have a social support network, you benefit in the following ways:

- Sense of belonging. Spending time with them helps ward off loneliness. Whether it's other new parents, dog lovers, fishing buddies or siblings, just knowing you're not alone can go a long way toward coping with stress.

- Increased sense of self-worth. Having people who call you a friend reinforces the idea that you're a good person to be around.

- Feeling of security. Your social network gives you access to information, advice, guidance and other types of assistance should you need you. It's comforting to know that you have people you can turn to in a time of need.

Healthy Relationships

Healthy relationships cannot happen unless both you are complete as individuals. Think about chocolate chip cookies. You start with a basic sugar cookie recipe. The sugar cookie is fine all by itself. Likewise, chocolate chips are complete just as they are. When you combine two very awesome things, you can get a third, equally awesome outcome. Relationships are the same way. Just like the vanilla in the sugar cookie recipe enhances the flavor of the chocolate chips, in a relationship, hopefully, you bring out the best in each other.

Activity: Chocolate Chip Cookies

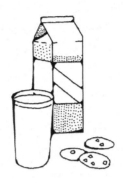

Start with a healthy relationship with yourself.

Think about how many different variations there are for sugar cookies.

- Make a list of your strengths. What "ingredients" do you have that make you totally amazing?

Then think about all the different stand-alone foods you can put in a sugar cookie to make it even better. (chocolate chips, caramels, candy corn, dates/raisins, peanut butter, walnuts, zucchini, carrots, Rice Krispies, oatmeal...)

- Make a list of what you look for in a relationship. Like chocolate chips compliment and bring out the best in a sugar cookie, what characteristics in a person bring out the best in you?

Just like there are some foods you just do not combine, not every person is a good fit for another. Think about stand-alone foods you wouldn't add to a sugar cookie. Examples: sardines (salty), hot pepper flakes (spicy), black licorice (funky), oysters (slimy), lemon slices (sour), kale (bitter), popcorn (would dissolve))

- Who have you known who has been spicy (angry, irritable), slimy (manipulative), sourpuss, bitter, or salty (abrasive and critical). These things will likely not bring out the best in you.

Use these lists to help you evaluate your relationships. Although few, if any people will fit all your criteria for an ideal friend, you want to strive to have people that more or less fit the description of what you look for.

Activity: Characteristics of Healthy Relationships

The following are characteristics of healthy relationships. Identify the five most important people in your life. (This can include children). Write down how you encourage or nurture each of the qualities in each of those relationships and in yourself (so you are making 6 lists).

Healthy relationships don't come easy. They require you to have a significant amount of knowledge about yourself and others. The following list is a synopsis of current thoughts on the subject.

Skills Required for Healthy Relationships

- Expressing open affection and loving thoughts
- Sensitivity to feelings of others
- Being sharing and open with your feelings
- Trust and honesty
- Relating to others with warmth and tenderness
- Listening, hearing and understanding others
- Being accepting and uncritical
- Ability to care deeply for oneself and another individual
- Ability and willingness to show respect for others
- Giving compliments and reassurance
- Being contentious and dependable
- Encouraging growth in myself and others

A relationship cannot survive on its own. It needs the care and nurturing of two people, giving to each other in a way that creates a mutually beneficial connection. This means that if you are down, your friend is there to help you up, and vice versa. Relationships that are only one way are doomed to failure (and to increase depression and stress in your life).

Think about which of these skills you have and which you may need to develop. I encourage you to read the book "The Five Love Languages," by Gary Chapman for a quick way to start nurturing yourself and others. He teaches about how different people feel loved through different actions. Some people need to hear the words or receive physical touch, others prefer acts of service, having a loved one make quality time for them or receiving gifts. Think about which of these makes you feel most loved. Which one makes your significant other feel most loved?

Activity: Nurturing Relationships

Review the following tips, and ask yourself, do I do this for myself? Do I do this for my friend(s)?

- Kind, constant, and honest communication. Without talking, your relationship will not survive. The more you communicate, the closer you will be.
    - How can you improve your communication with yourself about how you are feeling, your want and needs?
    - Name three people you want to start communicating with more.
    - Not all of your friends will share your same interests. You do not have to share everything with everyone. Choose what is relevant and meaningful to that person. For example, my friends with children who live in the city might be interested in something I learn about parenting, but could not care less about the 5 new ways I found to improve the crop yield in my garden.

- Faith and Trust. Open, honest communication helps you develop faith in yourself and others. Trust must be earned. First you must trust yourself and your own judgement.
    - Practice stopping to think before you act to figure out what you need, so you can start trusting your own decisions.

- Boundaries can be emotional, mental or physical. You feel how you feel. Your opinions are yours, and you define your personal space. It is important that you are able to protect these boundaries and respect other people's.
    - How can you be true to your feelings and thoughts, even when other people don't have the same ones?

- The willingness to work through difficulties and disagreements.
    - Within yourself, you will often have disagreements between your heart and your head. How do you muster the courage to do the next right thing? When you make a mistake, how do you forgive yourself?
    - With your friends, practice assertive communication and working through differences.

- A sense of humor, some fun, and a bit of distraction from the rigors of daily life. You can't spend all your free time "working" on your relationship-don't make it a hobby.
    - Make sure to get fun-time in for yourself each day.
    - Discuss what you like to do, where you'd like to go, and how you both like to have fun. Then go do it.

- Sharing life lessons with your friends.

  - When you discover something about life, or you make a self-correcting move, let your friends know. You'll be surprised by the positive response.

- Emotional support, validation, and compliments. If you don't feel that your friends like and respect you, there will not be a strong connection.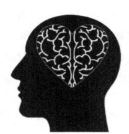

  - How can you do this for yourself?
  - How can you do this for the three friends you identified above?

- Sharing goals and dreams that resonate with both of you. Many people are happier when you are working toward a goal.

  - Make sure you always have something to look forward to and that you have someone to share it with.

- Compassion, acceptance, and forgiveness. These will show you the way through a difficult time. If you are friends for a while, there will be losses, challenges, mistakes and some things that you just can't fix. Weathering the storms together is a big part of what relationships are all about. Forgiveness doesn't mean forgetting or that it was okay. It means choosing not to hold on to the anger and drain your energy.

  - What grudges are you holding toward others or yourself?
  - How can you look at that situation more compassionately and forgive?
  - How can you better deal with your own mistakes?
  - How can you be more forgiving of others? Remember resentment affects you far more than it affects the other person. Ask yourself:
  - "Am I (or is he or she) doing the best I/he/she can?" If so, then it is not reasonable to expect anything else. Follow that up with, is there something I can do to help or make it better?"
  - What are three other possible explanations for why this might be happening?

- Unconditional positive regard. That means loving yourself and others for who they are, despite mistakes or poor choices. Saying "I love you, but I really don't like what you are doing." Remember though that just because you love someone for who they are doesn't necessarily mean it is good to have them in your life if they are continuing to make poor choices.

Assertive Communication

Being assertive is a core communication skill. Being assertive means that you express yourself effectively and stand up for your point of view, while also respecting the rights and beliefs of others. It can also help boost your self-esteem, feel less helpless and taken advantage of and earn others' respect. All of this can help with stress management, especially if you tend to take on too many responsibilities because you have a hard time saying no.

If your style is passive, you may seem to be shy or overly easygoing. You may routinely say things such as, "I'll just go with whatever the group decides." You tend to avoid conflict. Why is that a problem? Because the message you're sending is that your thoughts and feelings aren't as important as those of others. Your intention may be to keep the peace. But always saying yes can poison your relationships and leave you feeling taken advantage of. Worse, it may cause you internal conflict because your needs and those of your family always come second.

Now consider passive-aggressive behavior. If you communicate in a passive-aggressive manner, you may say yes when you want to say no. You may be sarcastic or complain about others behind their backs. Rather than confront an issue directly, you may show your anger and feelings through your actions or negative attitude. You may have developed a passive-aggressive style because you're uncomfortable being direct about your needs and feelings.

What are the drawbacks of a passive-aggressive communication style? Over time, passive-aggressive behavior damages relationships and undercuts mutual respect, making it difficult for you to get your goals and needs met. The internal conflict that can be created by passive-aggressive behavior can lead to: Stress, resentment, feelings of victimization and even a desire to exact revenge.

Finally, aggressive communication sends the message that your opinions are important and nobody else's are. It may give you the illusion of control, but people will often feel resentful over time.

Being assertive is usually viewed as a healthier communication style. Being assertive offers many benefits. It helps you keep people from walking all over you, and can keep you from steamrolling others.

Activity: Assertive Communication Tips

Pick one suggestion from the list each week and practice it.

- Pay attention to nonverbals—Practice making eye contact and not pointing or crossing your arms in front of yourself while you are talking to someone.

- Watch your tone and volume. Loud or rapid speech indicates either stress or anger.

- Think and talk about yourself POSITIVELY. Do this for a week, even when you are talking to yourself about yourself.

- Stop adding qualifying statements to your opinions or requests (e.g., "you'll probably think this is crazy, but…", "…I guess", "but that's just my opinion").

- Reduce tag questions (e.g., "Does that make sense?", "Is that okay?").

- Consciously take responsibility for yourself/avoid blaming

- Avoid taking responsibility/making excuses for others.

- Eliminate "should", "ought to", and "have to". Instead, practice using the phrase "I choose to".

- Eliminate "but" and "however" These two words just negate everything that came before you. For example: "I really like you, but…" "I know you need this done, however…."

- People (including you) are entitled to their own opinions/thoughts/feelings/reactions. Choose whether it is worth your energy to argue with them. This is true in real life, as well as on Facebook.

- Ask open-ended questions, that is, questions that require more than a yes or no answer.

- Shut up and listen

- Paraphrase as a lead-in: "I can see why you are feeling overwhelmed with everything you have to do…."

- Remember that "You" statements distance you from your feelings/thoughts/reactions and often put other people on the defensive. "I" statements communicate ownership. If you are talking with someone about an issue, start with "I am [feeling] about _____, because _____"

- Talk about the behavior, not about the person, and be as specific as possible—observable, measurable. Instead of saying "You are a slob." Say "I get frustrated when I constantly find your socks on the bathroom floor."

- Finally, practice recognizing the difference between something that is your problem from something that is someone else's problem.

Understanding Temperament

Temperament is thought to be an inborn characteristic that can help you understand how you prefer to interact with the world. While you are certainly able to function in a way that is not your preference, it takes a lot more energy. When you are depressed, you will often find that it is harder to find the energy to do anything, let alone function in an environment that goes against your preferences.

On the following page, you are presented with four dimensions in two columns. The column on the left can be viewed as one end of a continuum and the column on the right represents the other end. You will find statements in both the left and right columns that apply to you. Select the dimension that is most accurate. If there are a relatively equal number of statements in each column that apply, it means you are flexible in that area depending upon the situation. You can also go to http://keirsey.com and take the Temperament Sorter II for a more accurate picture and more information about the dimensions.

Activity: Know Your Temperament

By creating an environment that is most in line with your preferences, you can reduce stress.

By understanding other's preferences, you can improve how you interact and communicate with them.

For example, when you interact with people who have opposite temperament dimensions than you, embrace the differences. You are the yin to their yang. Neither of you is right or wrong, you just view things differently. By synthesizing the two points of view you will arrive at a deeper understanding of reality—not yours or theirs...just reality. You will need to compromise. For example, extroverts get energy from being around people and introverts can be drained by social situations. Finding a happy medium that helps the Extrovert feel energized, but doesn't drain the introvert is key. For example, my partner is an Introvert, and I am an Extrovert. When we have "get togethers" he can tolerate up to about 6 people at a time, and I get enough energy from only six people. He would prefer only one or two and I would prefer 10 or 20, but we compromise.

In the following activity, mark the statements that best describe you.

Environment

This dimension can help you understand the environments that give you energy and those that drain your energy (stress you out), and whether you prefer to do things alone or in groups.

- I like to know a little about a lot of things (E) OR I am intense and passionate, and like to know a lot about a few things. (I)
- I am generally very open and easy to get to know (E) OR I am generally more reserved and difficult to get to know (I)
- I like meeting new people, and have many friends (E) OR I have to exert effort to meet new people and have only a few very close friends (I)
- I think those who are reserved are standoffish (E) OR I think that outgoing people are shallow (I)
- I would rather figure things out *while* I am talking (E) OR I would rather figure things out in my own mind, *then* talk (I)
- I often enjoy background noise such as TV or radio (E) OR I prefer peace and quiet (I)
- I know what is going on around me, such as how other people are feeling and what they want rather than what my needs and wants are (E) OR I know what is going on inside me such as what I feel, think and want rather than what is going on around me. (I)
- I often do not mind interruptions because I am already somewhat focused on what is going on around me (E) OR I dislike being interrupted (jolted out of my "zone") (I)
- I am often considered a good talker (E) OR I am often considered a good listener. (I)

Learning

This dimension can help you understand how you and other people approach learning and problems---by focusing on reality, details and specifics or creativity, possibilities and the "big picture."

- I am practical and realistic (D) OR I am an imaginative dreamer. (C)
- I prefer facts and details and live in the now, rather than in the future. (D) OR I prefer abstraction, inspiration and insights, love talking about the big picture, possibilities for the future and "meta-concepts." (C)
- I prefer to do things to solve a problem rather than spend a lot of time just thinking about it. (D) OR I would rather think about all the possible solutions to a situation rather than take action.(C)
- I focus on practical, concrete problems. (D) OR I focus on complicated abstract problems.(C)
- I see the details like what I need to do for my health and may ignore the big picture such as the reason I want to be healthy so I can enjoy my kids and time on earth. (D) OR I see the big picture such as wanting to have an awesome life, but may not think about the details like what I need to do today to start creating that reality. (C)
- I think that those that dream a lot and are always coming up with ideas are impractical (like flying cars). (D) OR I think that those that focus too much on the details and specifics lack vision (such as how flying cars could reduce the need for land clearing for roads and would speed up transit to be able to get somewhere more directly). (C)
- I believe "if it isn't broken, don't fix it" (Cars work). (D) OR I believe anything can be improved (Flying cars could work better). (C)

Motivation

This dimension encourages you to look at what motivates you to get out of bed and what principles you use to make decisions.

- I make decisions based on what the rules, policies and laws say (F) OR I make decisions based on what is the most caring, or compassionate.(R)
- I respond most easily to people's thoughts (F) OR I respond most easily to feelings and values (R)
- I want to understand the objective principles like cost/benefit or likelihood of success (F) OR I want to understand how it impacts other people (R)
- I value objectivity and logic above sentiment and compassion (F) OR I value sentiment and compassion above objectivity and logic (R)
- I think that those who focus on feelings and relationships take things too personally (F) OR I think that those preferring objectivity are insensitive (R)
- I may argue both sides of an issue for mental stimulation (F) OR I prefer to agree with those around me (R)

Time Management

This dimension helps you analyze your time management style. Are you structured and punctual or spontaneous and a bit unpredictable?

- I always plan ahead and find unplanned events (even good ones) stressful. (O) or I fly by the seat of my pants, adapting as I go and find too much routine to be awful. (S)
- I am self-disciplined, purposeful and thrive on order, preferring detailed schedules. (O) OR I am flexible and tolerant preferring to-do lists to structured schedules (S)
- I get things done early, plan ahead & work steadily (O) OR I usually get things done late or at the last minute depending on spurt of energy (S)
- I am time and deadline oriented. (O) OR I always think there is plenty of time (S)
- I want closure and might be hasty in making decisions just to get it done and off my desk. (O) OR I am always looking for more information and may fail to make decisions for fear of missing last-minute opportunities. (S)
- I dislike surprises (O) OR I love surprises (S)
- I think those preferring spontaneity are unpredictable (O) OR I think those who are not spontaneous are too rigid (S)
- I usually make effective choices but may not appreciate or make use of things which are not planned or expected (O) OR I am quite adept at handling unplanned events, but may not make effective choices among the possibilities (S)

In the last section you will identify your LEAP subtype: Leader, Entertainer, Architect and Protector which can help you understand how to communicate with different personalities.

Leader

- I am motivated by competition and love to be in control and get things accomplished (L)   True or False
- I tend to be very direct (sometimes insensitive) (L) True or False
- I am described as high strung and strong willed (L) True or False
- I am described as outgoing (L) True or False
- I value competence over sensitivity in my co-workers. (L) True or False
- I need independence and cannot stand to be nagged or micromanaged. (L) True or False
- It takes a lot for me to be patient and sensitive to other people's feelings. (L) True or False
- In discussions I prefer to just get to the point and focus on solutions. (L) True or False

Entertainer

- I am usually enthusiastic, warm and optimistic. (E) True or False
- I value democratic relationships and popularity (E) True or False
- I am motivated by social recognition and relationships (E) True or False
- I fear disapproval and being ignored. (E) True or False
- When solving problems, I like to ask questions and ponder all aspects. (E) True or False
- I like to work in teams to get things done. (E) True or False
- I have difficulty focusing for long periods (E) True or False
- I get bored with too much structure and have difficulty completing large tasks. (E) True or False

Architect

- I work steadily within existing circumstances to ensure quality and accuracy. (A) True or False
- I am motivated by opportunities to gain knowledge and show my expertise. (A) True or False
- I am described as careful, systematic, diplomatic, and accurate. (A) True or False
- Sometimes I am overcritical, overanalyzing and isolate myself. (A) True or False
- I have difficulty letting go of things and delegating tasks. (A) True or False
- I struggle to compromise for the good of the team (A) True or False
- Social events and celebrations can be very stressful for me. (A) True or False
- I prefer when people focus on facts and details, are patient and minimize "pep talk" or emotional language. (A) True or False

Protector

1. When solving problems, I like to work alone (P) True or False
2. I am described as calm, patient and predictable (P) True or False
3. I can be indecisive and tend to avoid change (P) True or False
4. I value loyalty (P) True or False
5. I strive for approval from my superiors (P) True or False
6. I enjoy being in charge so I can get things done (P) True or False
7. I get stressed when I have to quickly adapt to change, or expectations are unclear. (P) True or False
8. I like others to be clear, but not confrontational, in what they expect from me (P) True or False

To find your personality type, go back over the assessment count your responses. Remember, that most people will not be exclusively one type or the other.

Environment preferences: Do you have more Es (Extrovert) or Is (Introvert)?   _____

Learning preferences: Do you have more Ds (Details) or Cs (Concepts)?   _____

Motivation preferences: Do you have more Fs (Facts) or Rs (Relationships)?   _____

Time Management preferences: Do you have more Os (Organization) or Ss (Spontaneity) _____

Put those 4 letters together to get your general temperament (EDFO, ICRS, ECFS etc.) _____

To identify your communication subtype, complete the following questions.

- How many True responses in the Leader category ? _____

- How many True responses in the Entertainer category ? _____

- How many True responses in the Architect category ? _____

- How many True responses in the Protector category ? _____

In which category do you have the MOST responses? This is your subtype.

Leader(L) Entertainer(E) Architect(A) Protector(P)

Repeat this activity for anyone you want to understand a bit better like your kids, spouse or boss.

Now that you know your preferences, you will learn a little more about how to use that information to reduce your stress and better understand other people.

Understanding Your Environment Preferences

Extroverts

Extroverts need to be able to be around other people and get lonely easily. They also need the opportunity to actively process information while they are talking about it.

Environment: Extroverts are very adaptable to interruptions and "open" and gamified work spaces. They also like large gatherings and parties. If they are working online or taking online classes, doing their work at a library or coffee shop can help make it more comfortable.

Career: They will prefer careers that work with others, and classroom style or collaborative online education as opposed to independent or self-directed study. Careers include: Beautician, cashier, sales, law enforcement, teacher.

Relationships: Popularity and relationships are a priority to Extroverts in a rich and meaningful life. When there is a problem, they often need to talk it out. If in a relationship with an introvert, they may need to write it down (or talk to themselves) or do something else for 30 minutes while the introvert thinks about it.

Important skills for recovery and wellness: include making a list of ways to handle "down" time so they don't feel restless or lonely and staying in touch with what is going on inside them (mindfulness).

Introvert

Introverts need to have quiet time each day to reflect and get easily overwhelmed by too much input. When faced with a problem or trying to learn, they need to quietly think about and process information without talking.

Environment: Introverts are very aware of themselves but not as aware of what is going on around them, so interruptions or interacting with a lot of people can be stressful. It may be important to take frequent breaks and walk around outside. They prefer small gatherings of one to four people, even for celebrations and "parties."

Career: They will prefer careers that work independently such as in a lab or private office and will prefer learning online and through independent study. Ideal careers include: Chemist, pilot, truck driver, accountant.

Relationships: Relationships with a couple close friends are a priority in a rich and meaningful life, but they will treasure their "personal space." When there is a problem, Introverts often need to have some time alone to think.

Important recovery and wellness skills include knowing how to prepare for and handle larger gatherings where they may have to "extrovert," being aware of the thoughts, feelings and needs of those around them and ensuring they set aside quiet time to recharge every day.

Understanding Your Learning Preferences

Detail Oriented

People who are detail oriented are very aware of all of the widgets they currently have to work with. They prefer learning about facts, statistics, processes instead of the theoretical concepts and philosophical aspects of things. They will put together a puzzle piece by piece instead of starting with the frame to get oriented.

Career: People who are detail oriented thrive in occupations such as accounting, management, copy editing, medicine, teaching and engineering.

Relationships: Detail oriented people can be off-putting to those who are Conceptual i.e. the big idea people. Both types of people are needed for any project to work. The Conceptual person has ideas about a new business, the perfect house or vacation or what makes a "good relationship." The Detail person will be the one to help identify all of the details and things that need to be considered to achieve that big idea.

Important skills for recovery and wellness include making sure to look up occasionally at the big picture and not get lost in the weeds. Asking "How is this helping me move toward or embrace a rich and meaningful life." "Why is it that I am doing all this?"

Conceptual

Those who are Conceptual people are dreamers and have difficulty with attention to details. They can see ways to improve just about anything and love to think about possibilities.

Career: Those who are Conceptual thrive in occupations where their creativity can shine: Photography, graphic design, author, grant writer, artist, composer, actor, interior designer etc.

Relationships: Being dreamers, idea oriented can be off-putting to people who are detail-oriented. Both types of people are needed for any project to work. The Conceptual person has ideas about a new business, the perfect house or vacation or what makes a "good relationship." The Detail person will be the one to help identify all of the things that need to be considered to achieve that big idea. In relationships with Detail people, those who are Conceptual need to remember that detail people don't want to talk about it, they would prefer just to jump in and fix it.

Important skills for recovery and wellness include making sure to consider all of the details—Who, what, when, where, why and how; learning how to accept that sometimes status quo is the best option and being able to effectively work with Detail people.

Understanding What Motivates You and What You Based Your Decisions On

Factual

Factual people are motivated by and base their decisions on facts, rules and laws. They are "by the book" people.

Career: Factual people prefer careers in which there are clear cut answers such as chemistry, crime scene investigator, engineering and business administration, and even law. They love manuals and procedures (even writing them).

Environment: Factual people will often be the ones hanging pictures by measuring and cross measuring, and will want things geometrically balanced and practical.

Relationships: Factual people are motivated by facts (cost of things, crime statistics, which options meets the identified needs the best, what the stated expectations are), and have difficulty talking about emotions. When solving problems, they often focus on the facts and the logical next steps. When they are with a Relationship person, they will need to be willing to validate that person's emotional reaction to things and use concepts like compassion and harmony to convince a Relationship person of something. For example, when looking at a house, the Factual person makes a decision based on facts like the mortgage, statistical safety, time to get to work etc. The Relationship person makes a decision based on things like what makes the kids happy, if they will have friends in the neighborhood and if the travel time to and from work will take away too much from family time.

Important skills for recovery and wellness: Be willing to consider the impact of things on the other people's feelings/happiness and consider compromise (sometimes the most logical thing to do to get what you want is to ensure the other person is happy). Be open to occasionally doing something just for the experience, not because it is logical. Get in touch with what energizes you (makes you happy).

Relationship

Relationship people are motivated by maintaining interpersonal harmony and showing compassion for others.

Career: Relationship people prefer careers in which there is the opportunity to help other people and work as part of a team. Careers include counseling, medicine, clergy, environmental sciences.

Environment: Relationship people are very sensitive to tension in the room and need to exert effort to maintain healthy emotional boundaries.

Relationships: Relationship people are motivated by compassion and, well, relationships. When trying to convince a Factual person of something, it is important present facts and logical reasons why it is the "right" thing to do. Relationship people need to talk about a problem and have their feelings validated first so they feel connection and support.

Important skills for recovery and wellness: Remember that, for the most part, you are not responsible for other people's feelings. While you may strive for harmony and compassion, some people may just have too many issues, and in the end, you need to focus on doing what is in the best interest of the people who are most important to your rich and meaningful life. It is also important to be willing to consider facts and logical arguments for things. Sometimes leading with your heart instead of your head can get you in trouble.

Understanding Your Time Management Style

Organized

Organized people are highly structured and deadline oriented. Organized people are often also detail oriented people.

Career: Organized people like order, schedules, deadlines and predictability. They do well in careers in which there is a lot of planning: Teachers, journalists, office managers, production supervisors, bank teller, x-ray technicians, pilots and anything with regular hours. They often prefer working sequentially instead of multitasking.

Environment: Organized people tend to get very stressed out if there isn't a lot of predictability or if plans change at the last minute. They will often pass up opportunities to do something if it isn't planned at least 24 hours ahead of time. They may have particular days for laundry, shopping, paying bills etc. They also thrive on order and get stressed out in disorganized or cluttered environments.

Relationships: Organized people are excellent time managers, but can seem extremely rigid to Spontaneous people. One compromise is to schedule in a day each week for "quality time." This way the perceiver can wake up that morning and decide what to do, but the judger is already in the mindset that nothing else is going to get done during that time.

Important skills for recovery and happiness: Organized people must learn how to handle unexpected events. Have a plan B, and if necessary someone who is more flexible who can help them see the options in the crisis such as if they get a flat tire, their kid wakes up with an ear ache or they get a new boss.

Spontaneous

Spontaneous people are often idea oriented (dreamers and big-picture people).

Career: Spontaneous people like to remain open and flexible and get restless and bored if there is too much structure. They do well in careers in which there is a lot of unpredictability like law enforcement, emergency room nurse, and anything with frequently changing shifts.

Environment: Spontaneous people are very flexible in their environments and don't get as stressed about order. They also don't mind multitasking and will often have three or four things going at once. When things change they often approach it with curiosity.

Relationships: Spontaneous people do better with to-do lists than schedules and can seem irresponsible to Organized people. They are indispensable however when something unexpected happens because they can think on their feet.

Important skills for recovery and happiness: Spontaneous people need to learn how to effectively manage time and compromise with Organized people. They need to regularly check what they are doing to make sure they are generally on that path toward a rich and meaningful life and not getting distracted by every squirrel.

Understanding Your Communication Preferences

	Task-Oriented	People-Oriented
Outgoing/Extroverted	Leader	Entertainer
Reserved/Introverted	Architect	Protector

When communicating with a EDFO-L, EDFS-L, ECFO-L or ECFS-L (Outgoing and Task Oriented Leader)

- **EDFO-L:** When communicating with Extroverted, Detailed, Factual, Organized Leader (EDFO-L) individuals, give them the bottom line, be brief, focus your discussion narrowly, provide details, refrain from repeating yourself, and focus on solutions rather than problems and have a plan. For people with "O" in their type, structure and organization is the name of the game. They will need deadlines and actual meeting times, not just "around lunch."
- **EDFS-L** When communicating with Extroverted, Detailed, Factual, Spontaneous, Leader (EDFS-L) individuals, give them the bottom line, be brief, focus your discussion narrowly, refrain from repeating yourself, focus on solutions rather than problems and be willing to brainstorm and leave things open-ended for a bit. For people with "S" in their type, flexibility is essential.
- **ECFO-L** When communicating with Extroverted, Conceptual, Factual, Organized, Leader (ECFO-L) individuals, give them the bottom line, be brief, refrain from repeating yourself, and focus on solutions rather than problems and be willing to make some generalizations, always consider the end goal/big picture and either have, or be ready to make a plan. For people with "O" in their type, structure and organization is the name of the game. They will need deadlines and actual meeting times, not just "around lunch."
- **ECFS-L** When communicating with Extroverted, Conceptual, Factual, Spontaneous, Leader (ECFS-L) individuals, give them the bottom line, be brief, refrain from repeating yourself, and focus on solutions rather than problems, be willing to make some generalizations, always consider the end goal and be sensitive to the fact that they may not want to make decisions right away. For people with "S" in their type, flexibility is essential.

When communicating with a EDRO-E, EDRS-E, ECRO-E or ECRS-E (Outgoing and People Oriented Entertainer)

- **EDRO-E** When communicating with the Extroverted, Detailed, Relationship-oriented, Organized, Entertainer (EDRO-E) subtype individual, share your experiences, allow them time to ask questions and talk themselves, provide details, focus on the positives. They are focused on harmony, teamwork, acceptance and need to talk things out. The EDCO-E will want to be able to clearly visualize the impact on other people and will want firm times for things like meetings and deadlines. They will need deadlines and actual meeting times, not just "around lunch."
- **EDRS-E** When communicating with the Extroverted, Detailed, Relationship-oriented, Spontaneous, Entertainer (EDRS-E) subtype individual, share your experiences, allow them time to ask questions and talk themselves, provide details, focus on the positives. They are focused on harmony, teamwork, acceptance and need to talk things out. When in a relationship with an EDRS-E be willing to brainstorm and leave things open-ended for a bit. For people with "S" in their type, flexibility is essential.
- **ECRO-E** When communicating with the Extroverted, Conceptual, Relationship-oriented, Organized, Entertainer (ECRO-E) subtype individual, share your experiences, allow them time to ask questions and talk themselves, provide details, focus on the positives, and don't interrupt

them. They are focused on harmony, teamwork, acceptance and need to talk things out. Avoid overloading the ECRO-E always consider the end goal/big picture and either have, or be ready to make a plan. For people with "O" in their type, structure and organization is the name of the game. They will need deadlines and actual meeting times, not just "around lunch."

- **ECRS-E** When communicating with the Extroverted, Conceptual, Relationship-oriented, Spontaneous, Entertainer (ECRS-E) subtype individual, share your experiences, allow them time to ask questions and talk themselves, focus on the positives and the big picture without getting too bogged down in the details at first. They are focused on harmony, teamwork, acceptance and need to talk things out. When in a relationship with an ECRS-E be willing to brainstorm and leave things open-ended for a bit. For people with "S" in their type, flexibility is essential. (Politicians fit well in this category).

When communicating with a IDFO-A, IDFS-A, ICFO-A or ICFS-A (Reserved and Task Oriented Architect)

- **IDFO-A** When communicating with the Introverted, Detailed, Factual, Organized Architect (IDFO-A) style individual, focus on facts and details; minimize "pep talk" or emotional language; be patient, persistent and diplomatic, give them time to think before speaking, focus your discussion narrowly, refrain from repeating yourself, and focus on solutions rather than problems and have a plan. For people with "O" in their type, structure and organization is the name of the game. They will need deadlines and actual meeting times, not just "around lunch."
- **IDFS-A** When communicating with the Introverted, Detailed, Factual, Spontaneous Architect (IDFS-A)   have your facts and thoughts in order; minimize "pep talk" or emotional language; be patient, persistent and diplomatic, give them time to think before speaking, focus your discussion narrowly but give enough details, refrain from repeating yourself, focus on solutions rather than problems and be willing to brainstorm solutions and let things set open-ended for a bit. For people with "S" in their type, flexibility is essential.
- **ICFO-A** When communicating with the Introverted, Conceptual, Factual, Organized Architect (ICFO-A) , always consider the end goal/big picture; minimize "pep talk" or emotional language; be patient, persistent and diplomatic, give them time to think before speaking, focus your discussion narrowly, refrain from repeating yourself, focus on solutions rather than problems and have a plan. For people with "O" in their type, structure and organization is the name of the game. They will need deadlines and actual meeting times, not just "around lunch."
- **ICFS-A** When communicating with the Introverted, Conceptual, Factual, Spontaneous Architect (ICFS-A) always consider the end goal/big picture; minimize "pep talk" or emotional language; be patient, persistent and diplomatic, give them time to think before speaking, focus your discussion narrowly but give enough details, refrain from repeating yourself, focus on solutions rather than problems and be willing to brainstorm solutions and let things set open-ended for a bit. For people with "S" in their type, flexibility is essential

When communicating with a IDRO-P, IDRS-P, ICRO-P, or ICRS-P (Reserved and People Oriented Protector)

- **IDRO-P** When communicating with the Introverted, Detailed, Relationship-oriented, Organized Protector (IDRO-P) individual, be personal and amiable, express your interest in them and what you expect from them, take time to provide clarification and enough details, avoid being confrontational, overly aggressive or rude, give them time to think before speaking, focus your discussion narrowly and on harmonious solutions rather than problems and have a plan. For people with "O" in their type, structure and organization is the name of the game. They will need deadlines and actual meeting times, not just "around lunch."

- **IDRS-P** When communicating with the Introverted, Detailed, Relationship-oriented, Spontaneous Protector (IDRS-P) have your facts and thoughts in order; minimize "pep talk" or emotional language; be patient, persistent and diplomatic, give them time to think before speaking, focus your discussion narrowly but give enough details, refrain from repeating yourself, focus on solutions rather than problems and be willing to brainstorm solutions and let things set open-ended for a bit. For people with "S" in their type, flexibility is essential.

- **ICRO-P** When communicating with the Introverted, Conceptual, Relationship-oriented, Organized Protector (IDRS-P) individual, be personal and amiable, express your interest in them and what you expect from them, take time to provide clarification of the big picture without too many details, avoid being confrontational, overly aggressive or rude, give them time to think before speaking, focus your discussion narrowly and on harmonious solutions rather than problems and have a plan. For people with "O" in their type, structure and organization is the name of the game. They will need deadlines and actual meeting times, not just "around lunch."

- **ICRS-P** When communicating with the Introverted, Conceptual, Relationship-oriented, Spontaneous Protector (ICRS-P), always consider the end goal/big picture; minimize "pep talk" or emotional language; be patient, persistent and diplomatic, give them time to think before speaking, focus your discussion narrowly but give enough details, refrain from repeating yourself, focus on solutions rather than problems and be willing to brainstorm solutions and let things set open-ended for a bit. For people with "S" in their type, flexibility is essential.

- How did completing this activity help you better understand why certain situations are more stressful or draining to you?

- How can you use the chart below to improve your personal environment?

- Complete the chart for 3 people who you are close to. How can you use this knowledge to improve your relationships with them?

Learn to say no (and yes)

A big part of depression is the lack of ability to find pleasure in anything due to exhaustion or a sense of hopelessness or helplessness. Many times you may be exhausted because you regularly over-extend yourself. You want people to like you. You want to be needed. You want to be…. whatever. In the end you may end up feeling exhausted and resentful, because the  activities spread you too thin, and the things you needed to do didn't get done. You may also be trying to change the unchangeable. There will always be things in your inbox. There will always be people and creatures in need. There will always be something, somewhere. You do not have the energy (or power) to be all things to all people all the time.

Activity: Priority List

Identify the top 5 priorities in your life right now. These are the things that are most important to you, and that are worth your energy. It is important to be specific though. For example, my number 1 priority is my children, but that is too vague. On the other hand, "Raising happy, healthy, responsible children" is more specific. So, when something comes up, I can ask myself "Will this help me raise happy, healthy, responsible children, or will it somehow cause them harm if I don't do it?" There are a lot of things that are neutral. For example, being a member of the PTA. Could that be helpful, yes. But there is no direct relationship between my children's happiness and the PTA, so I will likely choose not to spend my energy there. At this point, if you are exhausted, you need to be selective about the things you use your energy to do. Focus on doing only those things that directly contribute to helping you achieve your goal.

Activity: Mindful Time Management

For the next week, practice being mindful. Before you say yes (or no) to anything, think—"Will this help me be more the person I want to be?" or "Is this something I can afford to spend energy on right now?"

Sometimes when you get depressed, you get stuck in the "no" trap. You don't want to do anything. Part of being mindful is also asking yourself, "Is there any reason I cannot do this right now?" If you have time and can muster the energy, at least consider trying it.

For example, when I get depressed I don't want to go outside, but my husband forces the issue saying, "Just come outside and try it for 15 minutes and if you are miserable you can come back in." (I hate it when he uses my own techniques against me.) Or, you can propose an alternative that you would be willing to do. If a friend asks you to the movies, but you don't want to go, you could say, "I don't want to go to the movies, but I would consider going out for coffee." This encourages connectedness with other people, and helps you focus on the things you could do instead of those you don't want to.

Healthy relationships need to be nurtured but sometimes there are also blocks or obstacles that need to be cleared out. One block to healthy relationships can be "baggage" you carry from the past. This "baggage" affects your ability to become attached and form intimate relationships, disrupts your boundaries and affects your ability to effectively communicate with one another.

Activity: Baggage Claim

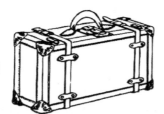

- List the influential you in your life: Parents, friends, past loves (and current ones).

- Identify what each of you has taught you about relationships (good and bad).

- Compare that to the Skills Required for Healthy Relationships above.

- Decide what baggage you have from each relationship that you are going to choose to carry and what you are going to learn from and let go. (It is not fair to hold everyone hostage because a parent could not openly express affection or one of your friends is not encouraging and supportive, for example)

- Identify what skills you need to work on.

- Focus on improving one area each week.

Pets

When you are depressed, you may get stuck in your own head. You may see all people as a source of stress, and have difficulty calming down. Research has found that petting an animal (bird, bunny, cat, dog, horse) can help you calm down, and reduce your blood pressure and heart rate.

- Pets are a wonderful source of unconditional positive regard. Your pets don't care if you are having a bad hair day or your boss was a jerk.

- Pets have a welcoming and soothing presence and can be good companions. Why do you think one of the highest uses of internet bandwidth comes from animal videos? Most people would agree that dogs are great companions, because they will cuddle with you, lick your tears and accept you no matter what. There are also certain cats who share that same demeanor. My cat Mojo can sense when I am stressed and will crawl up on my lap, put his paws on my chest and start purring. When I am not stressed, he brings me his toy and plays fetch. Maybe deep down inside, he is a dog. Rabbits, parrots and equines (horses and donkeys) have all demonstrated a similar ability to read and help their humans.

- Pets can change your behavior. You may walk in from a bad day, or just feel completely wiped out (depression will do that), and your best, four-legged friend greets you at the door. For at least that moment, you probably forget about all of the other "stuff" and play with your friend.

- Pets can help distract you. It takes some concentration, but when you stop to focus on your pet (or even videos of someone else's pet), it gets you out of your own head for a minute. This lets some of those stress and depression hormones subside.

- Pets can make you laugh. As you read about earlier, laughter releases endorphins which can help mediate depression.

- Pets can also get you into a schedule which can help reset your circadian rhythms. One of the symptoms of depression is difficulty sleeping coupled with fatigue and poor-quality sleep when you do get it. By getting up and taking Fido out, you are getting an early dose of sunlight which cues your body to wake up. In the evening, that last walk may serve as a cue to you as well as the puppy to get ready for bed.

Activity: Furry Friends

You may not be ready to commit to a forever pet, but you can foster animals who are looking for their forever home, or just go to the shelter and spend time with some of the animals who are looking for your new family. Petsmart has one of the biggest networks of adoption organizations, or you can log on to PetFinder to locate rescues in your area who might need fosters or volunteers. Rescues often cover the costs of an animal while you are fostering them. While it is hard to say goodbye when an animal gets adopted, it also means that your home and heart are available to save another life.

Spiritual

Recovery from depression can be a spiritual journey. It involves getting honest with yourself and others about what you can and cannot change, developing compassion for yourself and others and living mindfully, devoting energy to those things that are important to you. It is a journey that requires you to identify where you want to go, instead of aimlessly wandering through life.

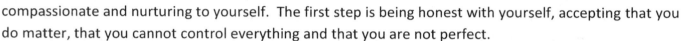

Spiritual maturity is a process, not an end. It is a relationship with yourself and the universe. Like any other relationship, it must be nurtured. You cannot fully experience this relationship until you can be compassionate and nurturing to yourself. The first step is being honest with yourself, accepting that you do matter, that you cannot control everything and that you are not perfect.

The next few sections will guide you through different aspects of developing spiritual awareness (if not maturity). It starts with remembering that you only have a finite amount of energy, so any activity you choose to undertake should have a *purpose* in your life. How does it help you feel more connected to the world or help you move toward what is important to you. Then you move on to living in the here and now. You may find that when you are depressed, you have a lot of guilt, resentment, worry or other "stuff" tied up in the past or the future. You cannot change the past and you cannot predict the future. All you can do is focus on doing the right thing in the here and now. What is the right thing though? Well, part of that depends upon you. These exercises will help you identify what your values are, so you can act mindfully and with purpose to feel more connected, and realize that you do make a difference which often relieves some of the hopelessness and helplessness that accompanies depression. (Why do you think "It's a Wonderful Life" is such a popular movie?)

Values Identification

All people have values, but very few people are aware of what their values really are. Values shape how you view the world, what is important to you and how you define goodness. Any of these can either contribute to a stronger sense of peace and self-worth, or a greater sense of confusion, helplessness, hopelessness and depression.   You are encouraged to evaluate: 1) What your values are, 2) where they came from, 3) whether you truly believe them, and 4) their impact on your actions and the resulting impact on you and society.

Activity: Identify your values

Review the list below and identify the values that describe you.

Acceptance	Diligence	Humbleness	Peace	Spontaneity
Accountability	Discernment	Humility	Perseverance	Steadfastness
Ambition	Discretion	Humor	Persistence	Strength
Assertiveness	Discipline	Idealism	Piety	Tact
Benevolence	Eloquence	Integrity	Prudence	Temperance
Caring	Empathy	Impartiality	Punctuality	Thankfulness
Charity	Enthusiasm	Industry	Purity	Thrift
Chastity	Excellence	Innocence	Purposefulness	Tolerance
Caution	Faith	Joyfulness	Reliability	Toughness
Cleanliness	Faithfulness	Justice	Resoluteness	Tranquility
Commitment	Flexibility	Kindness	Resourcefulness	Trust
Compassion	Focus	Knowledge	Respect	Trustworthiness
Confidence	Forbearance	Liberality	Responsibility	Truthfulness
Consideration	Forgiveness	Love	Restraint	Understanding
Contentment	Fortitude	Loyalty	Reverence	Unity
Cooperation	Friendliness	Magnanimity	Righteousness	Vitality
Courage	Frugality	Majesty	Selflessness	Wisdom
Courtesy	Generosity	Meekness	Self Sacrifice	
Creativity	Gentleness	Mercy	Service	
Curiosity	Grace	Moderation	Sensitivity	
Defiance	Gratitude	Modesty	Silence	
Dependability	Helpfulness	Obedience		
Detachment	Honesty	Openness	Simplicity	
Determination	Honor	Orderliness	Sincerity	
Devotion	Hope	Patience	Sobriety	

- Your values come from many different and often conflicting sources. How do you decide which principles to hold and which to compromise?

- Of the values you identified, which do you believe are important for you to be a good person?

- How do those values and beliefs impact your sense of power and happiness?

- Are any of those beliefs extreme? That is, do that use words like "must," "all the time," "everyone," or "have to?" If so, consider whether there is a less extreme version of this belief.

- Go back and identify the 5 most important ones. No cheating. Only 5. These are the ones that are your "guiding values" and are most important for you to not compromise.

Much of your stress, guilt/shame and depression may come from not living up to what other people think you should be (Their values). At the end of the day, you have to live with yourself. Other people can have opinions, but you need to figure out what will make _you_ happy (your values). Put your energy into that. True friendship involves caring about you for who you are, not what you do for them or whether you conform to what they want you to do. Start living by your values and being your own best friend.

Honesty and authenticity means being honest with yourself and others and making decisions based on your needs, wants and personal goals. Denying your feelings and always doing things just to please other people can leave you feeling trapped and depressed. What do you really want and how can you start living more authentically? (More about this in a bit.)

Honesty and authenticity means no longer lying to yourself and others about what you are doing, wanting and feeling and what the consequences are, living as you really are without having to hide from the reality of the past, or the present. Spirituality means finding yourself, learning who you are, how you impact your world, and how to respect and accept others. Not surprisingly, you may find it harder to be honest with yourself than other people. By ignoring your feelings, wants, needs, and desires, you may inadvertently be contributing to your own depression.

- Identify what you want life to be like 3 months from now. Be realistic. You probably are not going to win the lottery; however, there are likely a lot of things that could be changed or added that would help you feel happier. Nobody else has to read this, so be blunt about what you want and need. You can always shred it. By getting it out there you also have the ability to look at it and decide which changes are really what you want and worth making, and which changes are just knee-jerk reactions to stress or despair.

For example, some days I just want to run away to a cabin in the mountains with no internet or phone access and no responsibilities other than caring for myself. I would not really want to live that way forever. That is my knee-jerk reaction when I am starting to get burned out. However, I know when I start feeling that way, I need to take some rest and recovery time---and not feel guilty about it.

Now that you are getting honest with yourself about what you feel, need and want, it is time to start behaving authentically. That means acting in harmony with those needs, wants and desires. If someone asks your opinion, and you have one, give it. Don't say "I don't care," or "Whatever you want." There, obviously, is a time and a place to put your own wants and needs aside, but it is still important to be aware that you are making a sacrifice. Another example. I do a lot of volunteer work with animals. There are some days I would much rather just work in my garden or hang out at the gym, but in the bigger picture, helping the helpless creatures is more important. The same thing is true when you have children, friends, family or a spouse. (We all have at least one of those) Sometimes you will do things for people that you don't really want to do. You do it, because they are important to you. In those cases, putting your needs aside serves to enhance something more important to you. The challenge becomes balancing your needs with other people's.

Responsibility and discipline mean not only knowing what you want and need but having the courage to act upon it. Make a plan to start working toward a rich and meaningful life.

So far, we have talked about connectedness and honesty and authenticity. Remember that connectedness means becoming aware of your impact on others and your impact on you. Honesty and authenticity means being truly aware of and acting in accordance with your needs, wants and desires. The next questions are why and how. Once you are honest with yourself about what you need to be happy, and aware of how your happiness has positive effects on everyone and everything around you, then you realize that you have a responsibility to act in ways that improve your happiness and your surroundings and, indirectly the happiness and wellbeing of everyone and everything around you. Unfortunately, you are probably not used to putting you first and taking care of yourself. Realizing how much it can improve, well everything, can feel awesome, but also intimidating. It will take time, commitment and self-discipline to change the way you act and react.

Responsibility means becoming accountable for yourself and your own happiness without feeling excessively responsible for others. Feeling like you are responsible for how other people feel can be enormously draining, frustrating and, well, depressing. You are the only one who can control how you feel, and what you do with those feelings.

Activity: Responsibility and Discipline

1. Each morning get up and be honest with yourself about how you feel, what you do and do not want to do and make a plan for the day. (You will probably have to do some things you do not want to in order to achieve larger goals.... focus on the end goal to get through the rough spots).

2. Throughout the day practice acting mindfully. Stay in the present moment not worrying about something in the future or dwelling on something from the past. If you get distracted, bring yourself back on track. If you start getting into a negativity tail-spin---correct it. Put on those obnoxious rose-colored glasses. If you start feeling overwhelmed, take a break and get re-focused or re-organized. The key is to be emotionally and physically present and aware of what you are doing for the entire week. (Note: This will be frustrating at first, but once you start getting the hang of it, you will probably be surprised about how much easier life seems to be.)

3. At the end of the day reflect on your experiences. If you notice that there is something or someone who pulls you off track, figure out how to deal with it so you can stay focused on the present moment.

4. Finally, at the end of the day REWARD yourself. Do something enjoyable, even if that means just sitting on the couch, watching television and turning your brain to mush. Being mindful and present all day can be exhausting.

Tolerance and patience apply both to you and to others. Change takes time. It is important to be patient with yourself during your recovery. Likewise, if you are able to be more patient and tolerant with others, you will experience less frustration, agitation and exhaustion. What can you do to help you be more patient? (For me it is the Serenity Prayer).

Tolerance is the ability to embrace yourself and others in spite of perceived weaknesses or differences. Patience means to take events and experiences as they come without complaint or expectation, and understanding all things have a natural time and place to be. If you did the responsibility and discipline activities last week, you have had quite a bit of practice with being tolerant and patient with yourself.

Often both intolerance and impatience happen when you feel like you are out of control in some way. The traffic is too slow. The cashier is taking too long. The results have not arrived yet. This meeting will never end. Serenity involves both tolerance and patience and is the state of being calm and untroubled.

Activity: Tolerance and Patience

- Ask yourself, is this something I can, and am willing to exert the energy to change? If not, how can I change the way I feel about it?

Faith, trust and inner security help you focus on creating a plan, or Good Orderly Direction, and trusting that if you follow that plan you can achieve positive things. They give you the ability to live without anxiety or doubt, and with an inner security free of fear, worry and regret. How awesome would it be to not feel drained and overwhelmed by anxiety all the time?

- Who or what do you have faith in?

Activity: Trust Yourself

Before you can trust others, you need to learn to trust yourself. Yeah, it is hard. You may have been told your reactions or feelings were wrong. You need to start asking yourself:

- What do I want, and why?
- How do I feel and why?

Once you start to get reconnected to your own inner voices, you will be able to make choices based upon what you want and need, not what you think others want or need you to do.

Inner security, contentment and peace of mind come from the belief that what you are doing has a purpose and continuing to do it will lead you in a positive direction.

Activity: Inner Security

Now you will define where you want to be in 6 months, a year and five years.

For each time frame, answer the following questions:

- Where do I want to be living, working, and recreating/vacationing?

- Who do I want to be present in my life? (If you don't have many you to put here, identify what types of you you hope to have in your life)

- What will life look like on a day to day basis?

- Which issues that I have now will be resolved, and what will be different?

- How will my time and energy be divided among friends, family, work, activities of daily living (laundry and housework), and recreation?

Now, go back over each question and identify what needs to change to make that happen.

Your 1-year forecast will build on your 6 month forecast. This exercise is simply a way of helping you develop a map to where you want to go, or "Good Orderly Direction."

Wisdom and understanding can help you not only understand yourself, but also decipher the seemingly confusing behavior of other people, contributing to your sense of personal power and acceptance. Learning more about other people's spiritual practices and worldviews can also provide you new insight into questions you may not have answers to yet.

Wisdom and understanding come from conscious efforts to see things differently, to break out of habits and outdated beliefs and to creatively find new ways of thinking, doing and being. You may have never challenged your beliefs before. You may have not had exposure to vastly different viewpoints. Try looking online or reading about different spiritual practices for example, eastern religions like Hinduism, Buddhism, Taoism; Native American spiritual practices such as pantheism, and western religions like Christianity and Judaism.

You may not change the way you view things, but it will give you insight into how others view things. You may also find comfort in teachings from other spiritual cultures. It does not mean you necessarily need to give up your current beliefs, but you may add to them.

This activity challenges you to pick three to five spiritual practices or religions and compare them on the points which are most meaningful to you.

Activity: Spiritual Wisdom.

For the following 4 religions, Christianity, Judiasm, Buddhism, Pantheism, Atheism, identify what each teaches about each concept below.

- Love

- What is a sin and how do you get forgiveness

- Qualities of a good person

- Behavioral Expectations—What are you supposed to do (and not do?)

- Death

- Relationship to nature

More questions to think about...

- What similarities do the different religions have?

- What parts of your current spirituality give you comfort, guidance or direction?

- What parts do you question?

- What do you find intriguing about the other spiritual practices you studied?

- How can your incorporate that into your daily life?

- How can your spirituality help you feel less depressed, hopeless or helpless?

Gratitude, humility and willingness round out the spirituality section by encouraging you to remember to not get sucked into that negativity vortex. Bad things happen, but so do good things. Keeping the good and the bad in perspective can greatly reduce stress, depression and anxiety.

Gratitude is the recognition of the little miracles that occur every day. When you are depressed, it is easier to focus on all of the things that are not going right. If you adopt an attitude of gratitude, it can help you rebalance your impressions of things. There are 2 activities here.

Activity: Gratitude Journal

Keep a gratitude journal. Today I am/was grateful for… Try to write at least 3 things each day.

Activity: Attitude of Gratitude

Each time you experience something negative, force yourself to remember at least one thing you are grateful for. (Hint: If you keep your gratitude journal with you, just open it up and review it).

For example, July this year was pretty awful. I found out that one of my fur-babies had a terminal disease. Two orphan foster kittens I had died. I had to deal with a vindictive former employee. It was hot as blazes, and not raining, so my garden was suffering, and my best friend was supposed to get deployed. However, I am grateful for continued success at work; the health of my family and the rest of my fur babies, being able to live on a farm and not having to live paycheck to paycheck anymore.

Activity: Humility

Humility is the ability to move beyond arrogance and grandiosity toward an honest acceptance of yourself with all your strengths, perceived limitations and faults.   One of the reasons you may get stressed and depressed is by feeling embarrassed about things you have done or mistakes you made. Part of humility is realizing that your mistakes really are not that important to other people, and you are probably the only one that remembers them. The other part of humility is harder. It means accepting those things you are good at and being willing to ask for help with things which are not a strength. By refusing to ask for help you not only isolate yourself, you also miss opportunities to nurture relationships with other people and make it harder to get things done. By admitting you are not perfect, you also make yourself more personable to other people, and allow yourself permission to grow.

My son's first teacher was amazing with children. She was able to connect with them on a level that I was not, even though I had a doctorate in education (Hear the lack of humility?) Once I accepted that I did not have "it," whatever "it" was, and gave myself permission to ask for help, my frustration and self-pity levels went down dramatically. When I asked Jessica to help me learn how to connect better, it was positively liberating. To this day I strive to be more like her in my interactions with children. She is a great role model.

- What things do you need assistance with?
- How is it a sign of strength to ask for help?

Did you notice how the values for spiritual maturity sound a lot like the qualities of healthy relationships? Spirituality and relationships both involve nurturing connectedness.

Connectedness

Connectedness has to do with how your behaviors affect others and the environment and how others and the environment impacts you. A strong sense of connectedness not only encourages you to think before you act, but it also motivates you to act in ways that benefit you and those around you. The first step to being connected it to notice. You will never know how you impact others if you do not notice you in the first place.

Connection with earth, nature and everyday life helps us to feel less isolated. You play a significant role in the overall energy in your environment - each person can contribute positive energy or negative energy. People who enjoy their life work harder, make more money, have more confidence in themselves, have more friends and are far healthier than people who worry constantly, fight with others, feel negative or frightened all the time, abuse their health and have low self-respect.

Activity: Nature Walk.

Go on a walk for 30 minutes. Write down everything that you notice on a piece of paper—sights, smells, sounds, temperature—touch, even the little squirrel that was sitting in the tree. American culture often encourages you to try to maintain a breakneck pace. Ultimately, this means you may only notice the things that cause you problems, not the sweet, comforting or pleasant things in life. How many of those things do you think you would have normally noticed?

Activity: Mindful Awareness

For one week (or longer if it is helpful) keep a journal of all of the positive things that you observe, that happen or that you do which impact your day. My day almost always starts with driving out of my subdivision and seeing a variety or birds, cute little bunny rabbits and the occasional deer. The mornings that I can wake up and open the windows to let cool air in are even better. Try for a week, using stronger adjectives. Instead of saying it is a "nice" day, try "gorgeous," "breathtaking," or "unbelievably beautiful." Words like good and fine are blah and often communicate a lack of awareness and connectedness. When you have to search for a really descriptive adjective, you have to connect to the experience and really define it. Even if it is a negative experience, like a dreadfully brain numbing meeting, it helps you connect (and understand why you might be so drained).

Activity: Benefits of Feeling Connected

- How might being more aware of the positive things help you reduce your depression?

- When you are content, what is the ripple effect on the world around you?

- How does it impact:

    ° Your mood?
    ° Your relationships?
    ° Your patience?
    ° Your work?
    ° Your environment?

Activity: River Rock Exercise

What happens when you throw a rock into a pond? It makes ripples, right? It also raises the water level a little, scares the fish, and stirs up the dirt on the bottom of the pond. You are the rock. Your friends, family, job etc. are the water.

- In what ways do your actions impact everyone and everything around you?

Living in the Here-and-Now

Although it may seem gruesome to contemplate, none of us will live forever. When you die, there will still be things in your "IN" box, and life as you know it will continue to go on -- without you. Very few people will look back over their lives and say, "I wish I had spent more time at work," or "I wish I spent more time worrying about what others thought." However, you might say "He grew up so fast." "I don't know where the time went." When you are not living in the here and now, you miss the amazing things before your eyes.

Activity: Focus on the Present

Living in the here and now helps you appreciate what you have and focus on what you need to do to improve the next moment.

- What do you have going for you that is good?

- Look around. What do you notice? What do you hear? What is one thing you can do right now that would make you happy?

- How can you start learning to focus on the here and now?

Purposeful Action

You probably often spend a lot of energy on emotions such as worry, anger, frustration, resentment and being overwhelmed. What you fail to realize is that, in the big scheme of things, most of it does not really matter. Think about how much energy you put into dwelling on the last time you were embarrassed, or the last petty argument you got into with your best friend, or what you "should" or "shouldn't" have done.

Activity: Purposeful Action

Next time you find yourself dwelling on negative emotions or holding on to resentments, ask yourself:

- "A year from now, will this really matter?"
- "What is the worst that will happen?"
- "Is this something that is worth all of the energy I am putting into it?"
- "What else could I use this energy to do that would help me be happier and healthier?"

How would purposeful action impact those around you? How would it impact you? How would those changes impact those around you?

Environmental

Often overlooked is the impact that your environment can have on your mood. If you believe that your surroundings reflect how you feel on the inside, what would your environment be communicating right now? Is it controlled chaos? Is everything in disarray? Are you overwhelmed even trying to figure out where to start? Or...is your environment quite tidy on first glance, but quite different if you start looking in closets, garages, and drawers?

Cleanliness and orderliness are not the only things that impact your mood. Color and smell also have a great impact. Both of these are impacted by prior learning, but there are some general trends. Dark or intense colors may tend to intensify your feelings. Dark red for example can intensity passion or anger. Pink, on the other hand tends to promote feelings of compassion and friendship. Blue is the same way. A dark navy blue creates a much different feeling in a room than a bright electric blue or a soft baby blue. There are lots of books and websites ranging from Feng Shui to basic interior design that talk about how color impacts mood.

Three quick tips would be 1) use different colors in different rooms, 2) instead of painting the whole room one color, paint an accent wall, and 3) if you are not wanting to paint, try pinning up wall paper or adding colorful accessories like draperies, paintings and, my favorite, pillows.

No matter how orderly and colorful a room is, if it stinks, you will probably have difficulty relaxing and relieving depression. You will learn about different smells associated with relaxation, but you will also be asked to search your memories for smells that remind you of peaceful, happy or content times in your past.

Finally, to be relaxed, happy and productive, you need to be comfortable. This applies to everything from temperature to lighting and furniture.

Activity: Triggers for Happiness

Get 5 sheets of paper, one for each sense: Smell, Taste, Touch, Sound, Sight. Identify as many things as possible that make you happy in each area. See the examples from my list below....

- Sight: Pictures of my kids, rainbows, hummingbirds, sunshine
- Smell: Lavender, rosemary, rose, brownies, good coffee, chocolate chip cookies
- Touch: Cool breezes on a sunny day, soft blankets, my cats purr
- Sound: Favorite musicians, the call of a chickadee, silence
- Taste: Chocolate, perfectly cooked broccoli or zucchini, good coffee, cold lemon water on a hot day.

Order and Organization

Clutter and disarray cause you to waste time, disturbs the view of your house, drains your energy and may make others feel uncomfortable. Try this exercise--- for one week, before you go to bed in the evening, make sure the main parts of the house are straightened and all flat surfaces are cleared of unnecessary "stuff." How do you feel when you get up in the morning? How much time does it save you knowing where your keys and briefcase are?

Honestly, if you have children, your house is rarely going to be completely straight, but it is never too early to teach good habits. In our house, we have bins. Each bin has a theme: Star Wars, Transformers, Tinker Toys, Legos etc...You get the picture. I do the same in my closet. I have drawers for socks, undergarments, PJs etc. Keep things at least semi-organized, so you know where to find them. We probably have more "clutter" than many houses, but it is all neatly arranged in baskets, bins and drawers, so it is out of sight and not draining energy.

Activity: Say Cheese

The camera doesn't lie. Go around your house and take pictures then look at you. Does it look like a college dorm room after an all-night party? Straighten up enough that the camera is not able to find clutter. If you have children, post the picture of what "clean" looks like in each room so they know when they are finished with their chores.

Activity: De-Clutter

When you set about to de-clutter, you may find you do a better job if you just take everything and put it in a pile in the center of the room. Whittle down the pile over a couple of days. This way all of the flat surfaces and cubbies get a fresh start, so you can make tough decisions about what gets to stay out.

The Four-Box method forces a decision, item by item. To apply it, gather four large boxes. Label the boxes, "Put Away," "Give Away/Sell," "Storage" and "Trash." Take the four boxes to the declutter area. One at a time, pick up each piece of clutter. Ask yourself, "Do I want to put this away in another place, donate it (or sell it at a yard sale), store it, or throw it away?" You may not release your grip on the item until you have made a decision. At the end of the decluttering session, reserve 10 to 15 minutes to empty the boxes.

Box and Banish is an alternative to the Four Box method. Gather all clutter from counters, drawers, chairs, tables, floors, ovens, and bathtubs. Place the clutter into boxes or bags, and stack it somewhere outside the living area. Work until all surfaces are clear and clutter free. After 1 year, anything that has not been retrieved from the boxes or bags gets either donated or thrown away. (A few exceptions are made for memorabilia)

Comfort and Relaxation

Ahhh... the feeling of sitting in my favorite recliner or laying down on cool, freshly washed sheets. That is comfort. Ergonomics is important, but you also must be comfortable. As I sit here typing, I do have my back straight, but do not have my feet on the floor. I opt for office chairs that have arms which can be raised, so I can sit with my legs crossed. If you spend more than about 30 minutes somewhere, it needs to be comfortable. Your bed, work space, and lounging area/living room need to be comfortable and inviting. (Depending upon the person a cushioned toilet seat and footstool may also be important.)

Activity: Home Spa

When you walk into an office or room and have that---I am so relaxed I could stay here forever feeling, what is it like?

- Temperature?

- Smell?

- Colors?

- Décor/style? Modern? Farmhouse? English Cottage? Other?

- Furniture? Clean lines or soft and fluffy?

- Sound? Silence? Instrumental music? Music? Nature? Waterfalls? Other?

- Lighting? Do you prefer desk lamps, floor lamps, overhead lights? What temperature do you prefer your lighting to be? "Daylight" bulbs tend to be much cooler/bluer than warm white bulbs. Look on the packaging. The color temperature for cooler, daylight lights is around 5700K, while the typical indoor warm white bulbs are around 2700K.

This week create a space in your home (and if possible, at your office) that reflect these preferences.

Smell

Just like colors, textures and virtually anything else, scents hold special meaning for you based upon your previous association. The following are several examples of different scents and what they are supposed to do. 90% of reality is what we do with our perceptions, so if you believe that scents and fragrances have no effect, then they will probably fail to work on you. Likewise, your previous associations with these smells may alter the effects, for instance, you may have previously associated ginger with unpleasant feelings or exhaustion due to the fact that most people eat ginger-based foods around the holidays. Therefore, ginger may not work for you.

Application of aromatherapy involves either the use of a humidifier, atomizer or even spray bottle. Use great caution and seek expert advice before applying it directly to your skin and never take essential oils internally without a doctor's advice. Many are toxic. There are many websites and books that can help you discover fragrance combinations and mixing instructions.

Purchasing and mixing essential oils is often cost-prohibitive, messy and time consuming. A cheaper, less messy way is to try pre-mixed combinations of the essential oils (such as Healing Garden), or, for the more common fragrances like ginger, cedar and pine find you in your natural form, smell it and see what you think. When I was pregnant, the smell of a little ginger or lemon in heated ginger ale was the only thing that (besides eating jalapenos) that would stop my nausea.

There are literally hundreds of different fragrances. Essential oils are those which are derived directly from a plant. Fragrance oils are more commonly man-made. Fragrance oils are often much cheaper, but lack some of the therapeutic benefits of the essential oils. However, both fragrance oils and essential oils can trigger positive memories and feelings. Place fresh rose petals in a zipped, mesh sack in the dryer with your darks (just in case there is any color bleed). You will dry the flowers and freshen your laundry at the same time. Use pine cones to absorb essential oils and place them in a decorative basket on your counter (Make sure to cover it with lace, or mesh if you have animals or children, because ingesting essential oils can be deadly.)

Some scents are only easily available in "essential oil" form, other scents can be easily found in gardening departments, dry-oils sprays in the perfume department or ordinary foods. When possible, this is noted in italics. Scents that are in most people's kitchen cabinet or household are bolded.

- Angelica Root: relieves fatigue, migraines, anxiety
- Sweet Basil: brighten mood, strengthen nervous system, improve mental clarity and memory, relieve headache and sinusitis
- Bay Leaf: relieve depression and burnout/exhaustion
- Bergamot: balances nervous system, relieves anxiety, improves quality of sleep
- Cedar: calm emotions (try smelling cedar chips in the gardening department)

- Chamomile: sedative, relieves anxiety, improves quality of sleep (tea)
- Clary Sage: relieves stress and tension, improves quality of sleep, aphrodisiac
- Clove: aphrodisiac, relieve tension, worry, guilt and hostility
- Coriander: helps improve sleep, helps remove weariness and irritability
- Cypress: immune stimulant, increases circulation, relieves grief, jealousy
- Fennel: deals with mental, creative and emotional blocks as well as resistance to change and fear of failure.
- Fir (Balsam Pine): relieves anxiety and stress through helping ground one mentally
- Frankincense: Elevates mind and spirit, helps connect with repressed feelings
- Geranium: relieves fatigue, nervous tension, discontentment, heartache, fear
- Ginger: stimulates appetite, helps relieve confusion, loneliness, and nausea
- Try heating 6oz of ginger ale and adding 1/4 teaspoon of ginger.
- Helichrysum: helps you with addictions, grief, panic, burnout, emotional stress
- Jasmine: relieves depression, labor pains, and provides a sense of calm when dealing with bitterness, guilt and repressed feelings.
- Lavender: promotes restful sleep, calming influence
- Lemon: uplifting, helps energize and relieve apathy
- Lemongrass: helps relieve stress related exhaustion.
- Lime: uplifting and cheering
- Marjoram: promote restful sleep, help ease migraines, calms and helps relieve anger. Use as the moisture on a moist-heat heating pad.
- Myrrh: helps relieve lack of spiritual connection and emotional blocks.
- Neroli: good for anxiety relief
- Nutmeg: invigorates and stimulates the mind and helps regain focus.
- Sweet Orange: brightens mood, relieves apathy and burnout
- Oregano: energizes mind and body and helps relieve headaches
- Peppermint: improves energy, mood and relieves exhaustion (mints)
- Rosemary: improves mental clarity and memory, relieves headache
- Sandalwood: relieves apathy and melancholy
- Spearmint: eases nausea and headaches; energizes and relieves fatigue (gum)
- Thyme: relieves fatigue and may help with bronchitis
- Ylang-Ylang: aphrodisiac, mood brightener, promotes restful sleep, relieves anxiety

Activity: Aromatherapy

- Identify 10 ways to distribute fragrances (on a cloth in the sock drawer, on your pillow, in a spray bottle, lightbulb rings, wiped on ceiling fan blades etc...)

- Identify 5 scents that bring back happy memories or feelings of calm

- Identify 5 scents that help you feel energized and clear headed

Add these scents to your living areas this week.

Unplug

"And then! Oh, the noise! Oh, the Noise! Noise! Noise! Noise!
That's one thing he hated! The NOISE! NOISE! NOISE! NOISE!" {How the Grinch Stole Christmas}

These days it is easy to get exhausted and feel overwhelmed with everything. Employers and friends no longer have any sense of boundaries. Many expect you to be available 24/7/365. To top it off, you can easily get overwhelmed and depressed by just logging on to the internet (or worse yet, Facebook). There is always someone hurting, dying or in need. SO...UNPLUG

Activity: Unplug

Set some boundaries. Create an autoresponder for your email that says you will respond to messages within _____ days, but you will not be checking your email after 5pm on weekdays or at all on weekends. Then stick to that.

If you must use social networking, check it once a day, and limit yourself to 30 minutes or an hour. It is easy to get sucked in and lose a bunch of time. This lost time will only compound your stress and make your life feel more unmanageable and overwhelming.

Turn off your phone (or put it in airplane mode) when you are having "you time," such as when you are at the gym, in the shower or taking a much needed 30-minute break. There are probably a few people who need to be able to get in touch with you in an emergency. Consider screening your calls and/or letting everything go to voicemail after 5pm, then you can choose who you respond to.

If you find that the news depresses you, limit that too. Not much changes from day to day.

Final Notes

There are a host of causes of depression ranging from physical to social and emotional. Although you cannot have a stress-free life, you can take steps to minimize the stress you experience on a daily basis. By reserving energy, you are empowered to deal with life on life's terms. By focusing on what is going right and what you can change, you reduce the sense of being hopelessly stuck.

Made in the USA
Coppell, TX
20 April 2021

54159752R10072